# The ABC's of
# Personal Finance

## by
## Debbi King

# Table of Contents

# Introduction

*F* irst of all, I would like to thank you for getting this book. I believe that every word in this book can be life changing because it was for me. Many years ago, all of my bad money decisions came to a head and I ended up filing for bankruptcy. A year later, I found myself back on the same path. Then one day I hit my breaking point, and in that moment, I decided to never handle money the same or think the same way about money ever again. It took a lot of time, research, patience, discipline and prayer, but I was able to turn my financial life around and learn a completely new way to handle my money.

Everything that I have learned along my journey is in this book. The first thing I realized was that I did not possess all the knowledge necessary to make wise financial decisions. I was just doing the best I could and following everyone else. I also realized that I understood the math behind money, but I didn't have a grip on the emotions of money. Since personal finance, I learned, is about 90%

emotion and 10% math, I was in trouble if I didn't find a better way.

This book is going to talk to you about everything from getting out of debt to marriage to how your attitude can affect your wealth. This book is very straightforward and to the point. There may be parts of this book that you will be tempted to skip because you either think they have nothing to do with money or they don't apply to you. I am asking you to please read every chapter. I have had a long road and everything in this book was a vital part of my journey. I want you to have the same results and success I had in turning my financial life around. But to do this, you will need everything in this book.

You will see as you read this book that I am a person of faith. I will never hide behind that, but I want you to know that what is in this book isn't just for a person of faith. It is for everyone. It is about common sense. It is about making the right, wise choices for your life in the area of your money. It is about taking your greatest asset, your income, and becoming wealthy with it.

I am so excited for you to read this book. I know that if you read it and change the things in your life that need to change, you will be a different person in a positive way. Look, let me be honest for just a minute. I want you to be happy. There are too many angry people in the world and I don't want you to be one of them, but if you are stressed out about money, you will be. You probably feel that what you have been doing isn't working which is why you bought this book. Let my mistakes and journey help you. Be open to new ideas and new ways of doing things when it comes to your money. If what you are doing now isn't working, just try the things in this book and see if they will help you. It won't hurt you; that I know. Everything that I went through will be worth it if saves you one more day of stress and pain.

I don't know you personally but I love you. I want only the best for you which is why I have put my stupid out there for you. I truly hope that my mess can be a message for you and give you what you need to turn your financial life around. Only you can; there are no magic pills or miracle programs. But I believe in you. Now, let's go make it happen.

# A is for Attitude

Is your glass half empty or half full? Do you look for the black cloud or the silver lining? Are you a victim or a victor? You are probably asking what attitude has to do with personal finance. It has everything to do with it and every aspect of your life. Let me start out by confessing that for a good portion of my life I had a horrible attitude. I always saw the bad in every situation, I always blamed someone else for my problems, and I got angry about everything. Then one day, I saw my face in the mirror and realized how scary I looked and what everyone else was seeing. In that moment, I asked God to change me and over the course of a few years He has helped me to change into a better person. And my attitude was the number one area I had to change.

> *"If you don't like something, change it. If you can't change it, change your attitude. Don't complain."*
>
> *Maya Angelou*

As I go through life everyday and speak at events and work with clients, I observe so many different attitudes. What makes me sad is that there are a lot more negative ones than positive ones. Later in this chapter, I am going to talk specifically about the positive attitudes that can help you and the negative ones that are hurting you. But first I want to talk to you about attitude and thinking in general and how it can determine your destiny. I would like to share a finding that I discovered by an unknown author that has been very helpful to me.

### *Goodfinder*

Recently, a study was completed on one hundred people who were considered to be very successful in their personal and professional lives. All available information on these people was examined in an effort to find out what they might have in common. Finally, a universal quality was discovered.

EVERY SINGLE ONE OF THESE HIGHLY SUCCESSFUL PEOPLE WAS A GOODFINDER!

By definition, GOODFINDERS are people who look for and find what is good, in themselves, in others, and in all of the situations of life.

- ❖ GOODFINDERS look only for what is good in others and vocally affirm them, explicitly and gratefully appreciating the goodness and giftedness of others.
- ❖ GOODFINDERS look only for what is good in all the situations of life.
- ❖ GOODFINDERS know that the best blessings almost always come into our lives disguised as problems.
- ❖ GOODFINDERS know that there is a promise in every problem, a rainbow after every storm, a warmth in every winter.

If there is any gift I could give you to assure you a happy life, it would be to make you a GOODFINDER. GOODFINDERS are happy, productive, energetic, well liked, optimistic, enthusiastic and fun people to be with. GOODFINDERS help others become the best they can be.

## Are you a GOODFINDER?

By the grace of God, I can answer that question with a yes about 90% of the time now. But before my mirror moment, it would have been about 10%. A GOODFINDER is looking for the good in all areas.

* **Themselves** – Do you know that what you hear yourself say about yourself you believe more than what other people say about you? If you are always putting yourself down, calling yourself names and not believing in yourself, you will never be open to receive a compliment from someone else. A big example for me, as a Christian woman, was I had trouble receiving God's love for me because I didn't love myself. God loves you because He wants to. I now am able to say in every situation, good or bad, "God loves me and He only wants the best for me. Something good will come out of this. There is a treasure in my trial."

* **Others** – *"Stop judging my mere appearances, but instead judge correctly." John 7:24* Have you ever gotten bad service at a restaurant and

automatically assumed you had the most horrible waitress there? Just your luck, right? Did it ever occur to you that she was having a horrible day? That she was going through something that was painful in that moment? You should always find the good in other people. I am here to tell you that every person God has created that walks this earth has at least one good quality. And truth be told, more than one. Find it. We need to stop focusing on what we see and believing that we know everything about that person. Find the good in others, as you would want them to find the good in you.

❖ **Life** – You need to start focusing on the positive things in life. A huge example right now is watching the news. You have to try very hard to watch a 30 minute news broadcast and come away with a positive attitude, but you can. It is the job of the media to prey on the negative and fear in the world, but we can rise above it. For example, when the unemployment rate is 9% that means that 91% of the country is employed. If you are part of the 9%, you are going through a tough time. But what if your job loss happened to position you for a better job or to start your own business that you would never have started otherwise. My point is when life hands you lemons, you can either sit there and be sour faced or you can make lemonade. I hope you will always choose to make lemonade. Begin today to start talking positively about your life. Become a GOODFINDER!

### *Types of Attitudes – Good and Bad*

There are many types of attitudes that individuals can possess that can make them who they are. These attitudes can be either good or bad. Our attitude can move us forward through any situation and help us reach success or our attitude can hold us down and keep us where we are. Let's look at some of these attitudes – both good and bad.

❖ **Positive or Negative** – This seems basic enough, but which type you have can change your world. A person with a positive attitude is always trying to find the good in situations, just like our Goodfinder. They can find the treasures even in the trials. A positive person can go through the same situation as a negative person and remain happy during it

16

simply because of their attitude. A positive person doesn't grumble and complain about everything. They accept life as it happens and find the best way through it. A positive person will almost always make lemonade. A person with a negative attitude can hardly ever find the good in any situation. They allow their circumstances to decide their attitude and they grumble and complain about everything. A negative person almost always has a sour face. Are you positive or negative? Be honest and when you feel yourself begin to go negative, stop and turn it around. Even if you can't find the treasure right then, just say "I know there is a treasure here and I will find it. In the meantime, I will keep a positive attitude." Remember, you believe what you say most of all. So say positive things into your life.

❖ **Thankful** – It's hard to be negative while being thankful. I try to be thankful everyday, out loud, for all of the things I have, big and small. For example, I am thankful everyday that I wake up. I am thankful everyday when my car starts. And if it doesn't, I am thankful that I have the money to get it fixed. We have gotten away for being thankful for the small things, like running water, food, shelter and clothing. I have many people who come into my office looking for food and clothes because they have none. There are people in this country who do not have running water, shelter, or food. This is not a problem only in other countries, but right here in the US. I believe that if we can learn to be thankful for what we have, we will then be willing to help people who are in need. Below is an excerpt written by the author of "365 Thank Yous", John Kralik.

*"In December 2007, I had reached what I viewed as a nadir in my life. While my life seemed full of debts and disasters, I ached for the things and the security I felt I deserved. On January 1, 2008, as this dissatisfaction pervaded my thoughts, I took a walk in the mountains above Pasadena, where I was inspired to write one thank you note a day for the next year.*

*Although it took more than a year to complete the writing of 365 Thank-you notes, I continued writing them until 365 were completed. And then kept on. I learned to be grateful for the life I had, recognizing that the love I had for my children made my life already richer than the many people I envied. I learned to be grateful for my law firm, my practice, and for the love of friends and family that surrounded me. I became thankful for the many people around me who dealt with challenges far greater than the ones facing me, with courage and style. I learned to recognize the many people in my life who had protected and cared for me."*

This sums it up for me. Be thankful everyday for something or somebody. Remember, to someone, you are wealthy and have it all.

❖ **Entitlement, Greed and Jealousy** – All of these attitudes are very common right now and are a large part of the reason our country is in the position it is in. Many of the people today have an attitude of entitlement, which can lead to greed and jealousy. Do you believe that you are entitled to own a home? What I mean is, do you believe that no matter what your financial circumstances are or what your income is, you are entitled to a home? And not only a home, but a nice home. Well, you are not, and neither am I. If you want to own a nice home, you can have one by working hard, saving, sacrificing and a lot of patience. Let's say you have a friend who just bought a nice $300,000 home. They probably have worked extra jobs, stayed out of debt, and sacrificed and saved for many years to finally be able to afford this home. You, however, are in debt, have no savings, and are only willing to work as minimum as you need to pay your bills. If you believe you are entitled to the same home, you are wrong and very likely suffering from greed and jealousy. We always want what other people have, but we are rarely willing to do what they did to get it. I was a prime example of this years ago. When I graduated college, and got my first job, making $13,000/year, I thought I was set. I wanted a house, nice furniture, a nice car, and all of the things that I saw that my parents had. There was just one difference in me and my parents. My parents had worked hard for 30 years, living within their means and sacrificing, to have what they had. I had only just begun.

Greedy people are never satisfied. When we are never satisfied, we easily find things wrong with other people. *"The greedy stir up conflict, but those who trust in the Lord will prosper." Proverbs 28:25* If you are never satisfied, you will always have a bad attitude. You are not entitled to happiness but you do have the right to pursue it. Happiness and satisfaction are not found in things. God wants you to have all of the desires of your heart, but always remember, you are not entitled to them. You must make wise decisions and keep a positive attitude to prosper.

❖ **Wilderness Mentality** – This attitude is the one most of us have and the one that can cause us the most suffering if we are not careful. A prime example of this mentality is found in the Old Testament of the Bible, but could be found in many places today. In the story about the Israelite's journey to the Promised Land, we see that the Israelites were scheduled to make an 11 day journey to the freedom God wanted them to have. However, this 11 day journey took them 40 years and of the original 1.5 million people who started the journey, only 2 made it to the Promised Land. I have studied this story a lot because I find myself going around the same mountain again and again in many areas of my life. This wilderness mentality can be applied to any area of your life, but I want to focus on the financial area for now. Below are several wilderness mentalities that caused the Israelites to never see their Promised Land and perhaps may be what's keeping you from reaching yours.

1. **Their future was based on their past and present circumstances.** Put the past behind you. What has happened in the past is done. You must move forward. God put our eyes in the front of our head so we can see what is before us, not behind us. *"Forget the former things; do not dwell on the past. See, I am doing a new thing!" Isaiah 43:18-19.* You get the privilege of writing your own story. If you are in debt, you can get out. But first, you must look forward to what a life without debt will look like and know that it can be yours. Then make the decisions, as tough as they are, to do what you know is right for you to do. Remember, life is always out there and sometimes (most of the time) things won't go according to our plan, but never give up. Keep going forward.

2. **Somebody do it for me – I am not responsible.** This is a huge problem in our country today. Everyone believes that it is someone else's responsibility to get them out of their messes. In most cases, we have gotten ourselves into our own messes. Don't get mad – that is the truth if you closely exam the issue. No one wants to believe that they are responsible, especially for the big mistakes. Look honestly at your situation, be truthful about how you got there, and own it. Once you do that, you can learn and move forward. When so many foreclosures were happening in this country, many people blamed the government and the banks and they wanted to be bailed out. But in reality, many people bought a home without being financially ready. Many people fell for the "if it is too good to be true, it probably is" trick. This does not make them a bad person. It just means they made an unwise decision. And with that decision comes consequences. I know where they are coming from. I wanted so much, so fast, that I got in debt up to my eyeballs. But I promise you, the best decision I made was to

own my decisions and bail myself out. It took many years, but I did it. The biggest change we will see in this country is when people begin to take responsibility for their messes and go about fixing them.

3. **Make it easy.** It is never going to be easy. Life isn't easy. It took me many years of sacrifice and hard work to get out of debt and there was nothing about it that was easy. But it was worth every hardship. One great lesson that I have learned in life is that we can't appreciate things if they are just handed to us. We must work for them and work really hard. Many people never reach their dreams because doing so is hard. It takes commitment, sacrifice and dedication. You can save up to pay cash for a house, but it isn't easy. It is easy to sign a mortgage, but is it easy to be under stress for 30 years, not really owning your home? The answer is no. Do what is wise and best even if it isn't easy.

4. **They grumbled, were fault finding and complained.** Be thankful. Stop grumbling and complaining about your problems and do

something about them. The Israelites were receiving miracle manna from heaven every day to feed them and all they did was complain that they were only getting manna. They wanted more. Stop always wanting things you don't have and start being grateful for what you do have.

5. **Don't make me wait – I want it now!** This says it all. This is the slogan for debt. If you are in debt, one of the main causes is impatience. You had to have it immediately. If you want to succeed financially, you must learn patience. Remember the tortoise always beats the hare.

6. **My behavior might be wrong, but it is not my fault.** Then whose fault is it? How many of you love to play the blame game? That is a game you will never win. If you know that debt is bad, but you continue to use it, you are to blame. I, along with millions of my friends, are proof that you can live life, a good life, without debt. So decide to stop this foolishness today. And play a game you can win.

7. **Self-pity** – When something bad happens, do you ask "why me"? Have you ever thought, "Why not me?" For some reason, we believe that nothing bad should ever happen to us but it is okay when it happens to other people. Or we believe nothing good will ever happen to us because we don't deserve it. When you are in a bad situation, don't turn to self-pity. Instead, find a way out. Spend your energy in a positive way and you will yield positive results.

8. **Jealousy** – This is a mentality that is at the root of many people's debt issues. We want what other people have, but we don't always want to do what they did to get it. We have to have the newer car, the bigger house, the larger television, and go on the better vacation. Life is not a contest. The only way to win at life is to make wise decisions based on your situation.

Your attitude is an important key to your prosperity and your success. It is not too late to begin to have a positive attitude. You may be the most negative person on the planet, but you can change starting today. And as you change, you will see positive changes in your life and in your circumstances. Remember, life is going to happen and with life comes some good and some bad. But you get the privilege of choosing your attitude toward life. Choose to become a Goodfinder – today!

> *"Though no one can go back and make a brand-new start, anyone can start from now and make a brand-new ending."*
> *Carl Bard*

> *"We choose what attitudes we have right now. And it is a continuing choice"*
> *John Maxwell*

# B is for Buying a House

*A* home is where the heart is. A house is a possible location for a home. Those two words are often used incorrectly. Who you are is not based on whether you own a house or not. I believe that everyone who dreams of owning a house should pursue that dream with a passion. But I don't want that dream to become a nightmare. I have recently become an avid watcher of several of the house buying shows that are currently on television, but not for the reason you think. Most people watch those shows in hopes of figuring out what their dream house may look like. I became fascinated by the psychology of the house buyers. Almost every show, the potential buyers want a huge house with large, open rooms, large kitchens with stainless steel appliances and granite countertops, large closets and new flooring. Oh and don't forget the area outside to entertain. Most of the time, however, they are shocked to find out what size and type of house their budget will afford them. This is yet another example of us wanting now the things that our parents saved years and years to have. This chapter will not only cover the financial readiness of buying a house, but also how to wisely buy a house and get what you want.

### *Are you ready, financially?*

"I can afford it." This is a phrase I hear on a daily basis. But what does it really mean? I once heard a great saying. "Broke people ask how much per month, rich people ask how much." You see, many people believe that they can afford something if, in that moment, they can squeeze the payment into their budget. If a broke person makes $2500 per month and their monthly payments add up to $2000 per month, then that means, to them, that they can afford a new payment, as long as it is not more than $500.

The real definition of being able to afford something, including a house, is if you have the cash to pay for it. Buying a house with cash is possible. However, many people choose to take out a mortgage, which is okay as long as you follow a wise financial path when deciding how much house to buy. A mortgage is a risk, just like any other type of loan is, but a least with a mortgage you have an asset to back it up and you should be able to stay above water by following a few simple financial guidelines before and during the buying process.

First, you should be completely out of debt before buying a house. You should also have a 6-8 month emergency fund set aside. Once these goals are met, then you need to save up a 20% down payment. When you are ready to get pre-approved for your mortgage, make sure the monthly payment, with taxes and insurance, is no more than 25-30% of your income and is on a 15 year (or less) fixed rate mortgage.

Many of you are probably thinking I live on another planet because these guidelines seem impossible. You may also be thinking that if you choose to follow these guidelines, you will never own a house. But let me remind you that before the 1990's, these were the guidelines that people followed because they couldn't get a mortgage otherwise. From the late 1990's to now, the reins were let up and banks were encouraged to lend to people, even if they couldn't meet the criteria. Because of this change in policy, the foreclosure rate went up by triple digits starting in 2000. You see, even though the guidelines may mean you have to wait a little longer to get your house, the odds are in your favor that you will be able to keep your house as long as you want.

You may be able to swallow this a little easier if I explain the common sense factor behind the guidelines.

* **Being out of debt** - Debt is a risk. This will be covered in detail in another chapter, but anytime you owe someone money that you may or may not have in the future is risk. If the only debt you have is a mortgage, there is still risk, but the hope of keeping the house is higher if you suffer a negative financial change.

* **6-8 month emergency fund** - You are going to live in a constant nightmare if you buy a house and have no money in savings. Even if you buy a new house, there is always something to be done. If you have an emergency fund, then when something goes wrong, it is an inconvenience not a tragedy.

* **20% Down Payment** - You may be asking "Why do I need 20% down when the bank will give me a loan with only 5% down?" Having 20% down is wise because it will help you to avoid PMI (Private

Mortgage Insurance).  PMI will increase your monthly payment until your principal is at 80% which may throw you out of the 25-30% ratio.

* **Best kind of mortgage** - Always make sure when you go to the bank to get pre-approved that you know what loan amount and payment you can afford.  Banks are notorious for approving you for up to twice what you can actually afford.  And if the only loan you can get is an interest only, balloon, or subprime loan, you cannot afford a house right now.  If you buy a house for $200,000 on a 15 year mortgage (at today's current rate), you will end up paying $270,825.17 for the house.  If you get a 30 year mortgage (at today's current rate), you will pay $354,200.16 for the same house.  With a 15 year mortgage, your payment may be a little higher, but you will pay considerably less for the house and be debt free much quicker.

Always make sure when preparing for house ownership that you can handle your house, even in the worst conditions.

### *Should I rent or should I buy?*

Financially speaking, if done correctly, a house is considered a wise investment. However, you should only buy if it is what is best for you financially and what you want to do, not on the advice of everyone else. There are several situations that I always advise renting.

- ❖ **Getting ready to buy** - You should never buy a house if you are not financially ready, as discussed earlier. It is always wise to rent during the time that you are getting yourself setup financially to purchase a house. This could take 3 years or 10 years, but never buy before you are ready. Renting, in this case, is not your permanent goal. It is just a stepping stone to get you to your next goal of house ownership. It is also helpful to rent the least expensive place you can, with the mindset that it is not permanent. This will help you reach your goals quicker.

- ❖ **The wonderful men and women who serve our country** – If you are in the military, I always advise you to rent unless you are being stationed somewhere for more than 5 years. You do not have the luxury of staying in a city until your house sells, and then move. Therefore, you could end up becoming a long distance landlord by default and that is not what you want.

❖ **Newlyweds** – I know that all newly married couples are anxious to start their lives together and most of them want to do it in a new house. However, I advise couples in premarriage counseling to wait a year before buying a house. You need that year to get to know each other and enjoy each other. Living with your new spouse can be very eye opening. At the end of your first year of marriage, you will be more equipped to work together to find the perfect house for you.

❖ **Job change** – If you either get transferred by your current company to a new city or move to a new city to take a job, you need to wait at least a year before buying a house. Similarly to the newlyweds, you need time to scope out the city, to find the best school districts and to determine exactly where you want to live. You also want to make sure that you are going to be happy in this new city and your new job. I will always encourage you to move onto better things, just do it in a way that you won't regret if it doesn't work out.

- ❖ **Divorce and Death** – These are horrible things that happen to good people and the last thing you need during this time is to be buying a house. Again, in this situation, one year is a good amount of time to rent before making a large purchase, such as a house. And in some scenarios, it is okay to rent longer, even permanently, if that is what is best for you. Many adults don't want to deal with the maintenance of a house and the upkeep that they require. And that is perfectly okay. There is nothing wrong with renting in this situation.

These are just a few scenarios in which renting is advisable. However, you always need to make the best choices for you. Never do anything just because someone tells you to. You know what is best for you in your situation.  There is no shame in renting if it is right for you.

### *Which one?*

Now you are ready to buy the biggest purchase you will probably ever make.  But how do you decide which one?  We all have our wish list, but as you will soon see, finding a house with everything on your wish list will be difficult, if not impossible.  This does not mean that you have to ditch your dream of owning the house that you have always wanted.  There are many factors to consider when deciding on which house is the best purchase for you right now.  Let's go over a few of these and see where some compromises and solutions can be found.

❖ **Finances –** As discussed in the earlier section, you have to decide what amount of house you can afford.  Keep in mind, not only in this area, but in all other areas, that this house doesn't have to be the house you live in forever.  In some cases, however, this house can be a foundation for building your dream house, little by little.  My parents are a great example of this.  They bought their first home a year or so after getting married. They had a great down payment and paid off that home in less than 10 years. Then, they took that equity and some additional savings and bought their current home, which they have been in for 41 years. They found a home in a great neighborhood that had a good foundation. Then, over the years, they have made it their dream home. They have been mortgage free for the last 31 years. Just imagine what that would be like. So whether this house is a stepping stone for you or your dream house, don't take on more than you can handle in this moment. I promise that when you have the financial ability to move up in house, there will be plenty of houses to choose from.

❖ **Focus on the 3 L's not the 3 C's –** As I mentioned earlier, I watch some of the house shows on television and I have noticed a common problem, especially with first time house buyers. The buyers tend to focus on the things that can be changed and not on the things that can't. When you are looking for a house, you need to focus on location, layout and lot. These are areas that cannot be changed in a house. These may be areas where compromise and acceptance are necessary, but remember these cannot be changed. If you want a large backyard, and your budget will only afford you a small backyard, then you will have to decide to accept this for a while or postpone your house buying until you have more money. But also understand, if a big backyard is really important to you, then you will need to be patient and wait until you can find that feature in your price limit. A lot of buyers tend to focus first on colors, cleanliness and condition. In most cases, these can be changed. But let me add the caveat that cleanliness and condition are important to the integrity of the house. They can be fixed, but can also be indicators of how well the house has been maintained.

❖ **Foreclosures and Short Sales** – At the time that this book is being written, there are many foreclosures and short sales on the market. Price wise they can be good deals and should be considered. But there are also special terms with these kinds of sales that you should be aware of.

o A foreclosure is a house that the bank has taken possession of because the owner defaulted on their payments. These houses are often damaged and have items missing because the previous owners were not concerned about the condition. When you want to put an offer in on a foreclosure, you will be dealing directly with the bank. For this reason, getting your offer approved can take several months.

o A short sale is when the owner is trying to sell the house for less than they owe. When putting an offer in on a short sale, you will not only need the seller to approve it, but also the bank. Again, this can take several months.

In both cases, it can be an opportunity to get a great house at a bargain, but you will need to have a lot of patience and in some cases, extra cash to fix some of the cosmetic problems that come with this type of sale.

There are a lot of factors to consider when buying a house. It is also a huge commitment and responsibility to own a house and should not be taken lightly. I will say it one more time. I believe that everyone who dreams of owning a house can own a house. With wise financial goals and patience, anyone can own a house. But always make sure that your dreams don't become your nightmares.

# C is for Cash

*W*hen we think of cash, many times we think simply of money in the form of banknotes and coins. But to me, cash is a liquid asset that you can use right away if you need to pay for something. This asset can be in the form of money, a check, or a debit card. Basically, cash is money that you literally have. Cash is not a credit line on a credit card or money that you have promised to give to someone else in the form of debt owed. Before the 1950's, everything was paid in cash. If you didn't have the money, you didn't get it. There were some small mortgages but there were no credit cards or loans for small purchases. Some people might have a line of credit with a local store but that was only given based on your honesty and dependability. If you wanted a car, you saved up and paid cash for it. If you wanted a television, you saved up and paid cash for it. This philosophy meant that many homes didn't have some of the new inventions that were available right away. They had to wait until they could afford them.  This also meant that most families had one car, not a car for every person.

Unfortunately, with the advancement of technology and innovation, has also come the enlargement of debt.  We will discuss debt in the next chapter in detail, but it is important to distinguish the difference between cash and debt.  Cash is money that is yours and not promised to other people.  What would a cash only household look like today?  Let's take a look and see.

### A Cash Only Household

Below is an average budget of a cash only household for a year:

Income                                         $ 37,500
    *(USA Today avg income 2011 minus taxes – 25%)

Expenses:

| | |
|---|---|
| House (based on 25% of take home pay) | $ 9,500 |
| Food | $ 6,500 |
| Clothing | $ 600 |
| Electric | $ 2,400 |

| | |
|---|---|
| Utilities (telephone, cable, etc) | $ 1,200 |
| Insurance – Health, Life and Auto | $ 4,500 |
| Cell Phone | $ 600 |
| Gas for Transportation | $ 3,120 |
| Charity | $ 3,750 |
| | |
| Total Expenses | $ 32,170 |
| | |
| Cash Left Over for Emergencies and Savings | $ 5,330 |

This budget is based on a household spending only on necessities and having no debt except for a mortgage. This scenario is only plausible if the household has never incurred debt, which is always best, or has made the decision to get out of debt and is now living debt free. If you noticed, I did make an allowance for a cell phone, but for only one per household. This is because it is not necessary for everyone to have a cell phone. Cell phones were designed for emergencies when you are away from home, not as a toy that everyone must have. This is an example of being honest about the true difference in a need and a want. This will be discussed in detail in a future chapter.

Even with this bare bones budget, there is not a lot of money left over at the end of the year for savings and one large emergency could wipe everything out. But at least they have some extra cash to use and to invest for their future. Now imagine this same scenario with debt. Do you realize that one car payment of $425 per month (which is $50 below the national average) would leave you with nothing left over?

It became very clear to me many years ago that the only hope I had of ever being able to retire and enjoy my life was to go back to grandma's way of living (and mama's). I reevaluated my needs and my wants. I learned to wait for my wants until I saved up the cash to buy them. And do you know what happened more times than not? I ended up changing my mind about what I wanted. I also found that when you save up and pay cash for things, you end up with less regret. I was always buying things with money I didn't have and sometimes, even before I got home, I was regretting that purchase.

Do you ever dream of a life without debt? Even if you currently have debt, that life is possible and it is never too late. But you must take the first step and that is to stop incurring more debt and begin a cash only life.

## Envelope System

One huge step to beginning a cash only life is to incorporate an envelope system into your life. This is something that you can start today. Many people think that paying with a debit card is the same as paying with cash. Well, it is except for one missing element – pain. It is very easy to make your purchase, swipe your card and move on. But I have discovered that paying with cash has a certain reality to it. It helps me to think before I buy and to pay more attention to prices.

An envelope system is just what it says – using envelopes to separate and keep track of your cash spending. In our example budget, you would pay all of your fixed bills with a check, direct pay, or online. But with your every week expenses, you would use the envelope system. Using our example, food, clothing, and gas should be paid in cash. Our food budget is $125 per week. Therefore, we would take $125 in cash and put it in an envelope. Then any food we buy that week would be paid for out of that envelope. Once the cash is gone, you are done until the next week. There are several benefits to this. It keeps you on a cash based system (only buying what you have the money to buy), it keeps you in bounds with your spending plan, and it prevents any mistakes in recordkeeping, such as forgetting to log a purchase in your bank book. I challenge you to incorporate an envelope system into your finances and see how much more in control you will feel.

### *Debit Cards*

It is always better to use cash anywhere you can for the reasons discussed in the previous section. However, there are situations when you need to use a debit card where cash is not easily accepted.

One of the biggest reasons given to me for not closing and cutting up credit cards is "what if I need it." I am walking proof that you can live life without a credit card. "But Debbi, what if I need to rent a car?" "But Debbi, what if I am staying at a hotel?" Let me help you with the "buts".

All debit cards issued by banks have on them either a Visa or a MasterCard logo and they can be used anywhere Visa and MasterCard are accepted. This is because debit cards have two functions. They can be used as a debit or ATM card which requires a PIN number and can only be processed where debit cards are accepted or they can be processed as a credit card, using your signature as verification. When you are using your debit card as a credit card and you process it through the Visa or MasterCard system, you have the same protection as a credit card against fraud and unauthorized charges. At this current time, both Visa and MasterCard are offering "Zero Liability" coverage, which means that you are not responsible for any purchases not made by you.

All car rental companies and hotels accept debit cards when used as Visa or MasterCard. Every car rental company is different, but generally they put a hold of either a certain amount minimum or a certain amount over the total rental cost. For example, when I rent from my local Enterprise, they either put a $250 charge through or $100 over my total rental cost. When I bring the car back, I receive an immediate credit for the money not used. By the way, this is the same policy as when you use a credit card. Hotels work the same way. They usually put a hold on your account for a small amount above your estimated total. Once the actual charge is processed, the extra hold goes away. Again, this is the same policy as when you use a credit card.

The biggest change when going from using a credit card to using a debit card is the cash factor. You feel it right away because it comes from your checking account (your available cash) not from a line of credit you have been given. But once your transaction is complete, it is done. You won't be waiting for the bill, worrying about how to pay for it, and you won't pay extra for the item with interest charges. With a debit card it is done and done.

### *Emergency Fund*

My daughter is a Girl Scout and they teach you to always be prepared. This should be your personal finance motto. As I have said already, and will say several more times, life is going to happen to you. You cannot outrun life, no matter how hard you try. If you own a car, it will break down or need maintenance. If you own a house, it will need repairs and maintenance. I am not being negative, just speaking the truth. But if you are prepared for these emergencies, they will only be inconveniences not life changing moments.

I had a client once, we'll call her Mary, and she was at a point in her life where everything came crashing down at once. She had moved here from another state to get away from an abusive husband, she didn't have any family or friends she could depend on, and her self esteem and self worth were very low. She did have a job, but she was living paycheck to paycheck. Then it happened, the straw that broke her camel's back. She totaled her car and did not have the proper insurance to cover the vehicle since the accident was her fault.

So here she was, in a new town, no one to turn to, and broke. She did not have any extra money at all. The stress from everything that was happening made her very desperate and drove her to make a decision that otherwise she would have never made. She took $2000 from the company she was working for in order to get a car. She intended to put it back before anyone noticed, but she couldn't come up with the money to put it back quick enough. The company found out, fired her and had her arrested.

Mary has since repaid the money and turned her life around and used her experience to help others. I wanted to share her story to show you how important having an emergency fund is. You are probably saying "I would never do that no matter how desperate I got", but you don't know what you would do in her shoes. I am sharing Mary's story in hopes that you will never be in her shoes.

For many years, the industry standard has been to recommend a 3 to 6 month emergency fund. However, I, along with many of my colleagues, now recommend 6 to 8 months or more. The emergency fund should be, at a minimum, 6 months worth of expenses. There are a few get out of debt plans that suggest you do a small emergency fund first, get out of debt, and then save for the larger emergency fund. I would have agreed with this a few years ago. However, in most cases, $1000 to $1500 will not last very long and in many cases will not be enough. For example, if you own a house, one repair would wipe that out and more. Also, job stability isn't what it used to be. No job is guaranteed. You should always be prepared. I want to clarify that being prepared is wisdom. It is not having a negative attitude and always waiting for the other shoe to drop. I would highly recommend that you get at least a 3 to 6 month emergency fund in place before getting out of debt. You will then be able to concentrate more and make quick strides in attacking your debts and paying them off.

Also, make sure that your emergency fund is kept in a separate savings or money market account. You want it to be separate from your checking account, but you want to be able to access it if and when that emergency arises. You are not trying to make money on this money. You are simply setting it aside for emergencies, and only emergencies. By the way, a vacation is not an emergency. This fund is only to be used in actual emergencies.

As I am sitting here finishing this chapter, my car is over at the mechanic getting worked on. As I was traveling today, my car overheated once when I was sitting still. I was able to drive it home safely and immediately took it to my mechanic. They checked out a few things with me there and showed me that the radiator fans were shorted out. They advised me that I could hop along and showed me what to try if it did it again. But I had the pleasure and relief of telling them to go ahead and fix it now. Living a cash financial life and having an emergency fund gave me a freedom that, for most of my life, I didn't have. There was a time in my life that I would have been stressed about the $300 it cost to fix the car, I would have been stressed about driving the car and wondering if it would break down before I could get the money, and I would have been stressed for weeks after trying to play catch up on the bills I didn't pay because of the repair.

Money cannot buy you happiness, but it can afford you the freedom you need to take care of the things in life that will come up.

> *"Debt is dumb.  Cash is king."*
>
> *Dave Ramsey*

# D is for Debt

*D*ebt. It is an ugly four letter word. If I were to ask anyone who is in debt "Do you want to be debt free?" they would say yes. I don't believe I have ever heard of anyone who loves debt and wants to stay in debt. Yet here we are. Over 75% of the country is in debt of some kind. This not only includes credit card debt, but mortgages, student loans and car loans. As a nation, we have become comfortable with debt. It has become the norm to use debt to obtain the things that we want. I have found that the majority of the country believes that they can't survive without using debt. Yet, when asked the question, they want to be debt free.

Do you want to be wealthy? You will never become wealthy and keep debt. Wealthy people do not have debt. The cynics are probably saying "Well, of course they don't have debt. They have money." But how do you think they got that money? 80% of millionaires are first generation, meaning they earned it. But the key is they kept what they earned and invested it. They didn't give it away to banks and financial institutions. Deuteronomy 8:18 says that God gives to all of us the ability to produce wealth. This means that all of us can be wealthy when the money that is given to us is used properly. But if we are wasteful and unwise with what is given, we will not become wealthy. There are over 500 verses pertaining to money in the Bible and none of them say that debt is ok. As a matter of fact, many of them are very clear that debt is not wise.

In "Wealth – Is It Worth It?", S. Truett Cathy, founder of Chick-fil-A, states that wealth is worth it "if it is earned honestly, spent wisely, saved responsibly, and given generously." If you want to become something, the best way to do that is to study people who are what you want to be and do what they do. So if you want to become wealthy, study people like Mr. Cathy and do what they did. You will find that debt was not part of the formula.

The first step in becoming debt free and beginning your journey on the road to wealth is to stop all debt. You will never move forward in your journey if you continue to use debt. This is where the last chapter will come in very handy. In order to stop using debt, you will need to set up your finances on a cash only basis. Remember, this means that if you don't have the cash, you can't have the item right now. This applies to everything, from cars to vacations to clothes. It is at this time that you will probably need to introduce a new word into your vocabulary. It is a very painful word, yet is only two letters. No! The great thing about the word no is it only has to be a temporary word. For example, you may have to say no to a big vacation this year, but going forward you will be able to have nice vacations, paying cash, and enjoying them even more.

If you have always used debt, it will be hard to stop using it. Debt can become a habit. Many people use debt without even realizing what they are doing. Those same people believe that the answer is more money, when the real answer is no debt. Habits can be changed, as we will see in a future chapter. But you have to decide you want to change your habits. I have counseled many people who want so desperately to get out of debt. In the beginning, they are 100% on board. They even make the necessary changes, such as going to cash only finances. We make a few changes in their decisions and their budget and all of the sudden they have money left over at the end of the month that they didn't have before. At this point, many times, I lose them. I lose them because they were not ready to make the sacrifices needed to get out of debt. To them, it was easier to stay in debt than to make a few changes. Every time this happens, it breaks my heart, but then I remember, I was there once. I had to hit bottom, big time, before I said I have had enough. I will never go back to that life, financially speaking, again. I hope that by the end of this book, you will be there to. I want you to have your aha moment before you hit the bottom.

### What is debt?

*In Romans 13:8, Paul states "Let no debt remain outstanding."* You cannot get rid of debt if you are unaware of what debt is. Webster's definition is very simple – something owed. And it is that simple. If you borrow $5.00 from a friend, you are in debt to that friend until you pay it back. But I learned a little bit more about the definition of debt. Debt is a promise that you are making that you are not absolutely sure you can keep. When you take out a car loan for 5 years, you are promising to pay the lender, for example, $350 per month for 60 months. But how can you make that promise when you don't know what will happen over the next 60 months?  You are making a future promise based on current circumstances and we all know circumstances are constantly changing.  Most people have good intent.  We have every intention of paying it back, but sometimes our intent isn't good enough.  When many of the people in foreclosure bought their houses, they never believed that they would lose their jobs.  But they did.  And if they were not financially prepared with an emergency fund, they ended up losing their houses.

Debt is just a symptom of a bigger problem.  The most common problems that bring on debt are lack of discipline and lack of patience.  Discipline is planning your pleasure and your pain.  It takes a lot of discipline and patience to wait until you save up the cash to make a purchase, especially larger purchases such as cars, houses and education.   Let's say you want to buy a new car for $17,000.  If you finance the car, after putting $2000 down, you will end up paying $19,658 for the car.  This is at a 6% interest rate (the average as of today) and for 60 months.  Your monthly payment will be $321.  You will be in debt for this car for 60 months and will be paying $2,658 more for the convenience of having it now.  Also, if you get tired of this car before the 60 months is up, you will probably lose money in the trade and end up carrying that over to your next loan.

Now, let's see what buying a $17,000 car would look like if you had a little patience. First, you take the $2000 and buy an estate sale car for now. A estate sale car is ugly but well maintained. Remember, this is only temporary. Every month for a year, you set aside the $321 you would have made in a car payment and by the end of the year you have $4000. At that time, you can sell your $2000 car and move up to a $6000. By the end of year two, you can sell your $6000 car and get a $10,000 car. By the end of year three, you can sell your $10,000 car and get a $14,000 car. And finally in just four years, you can sell your $14,000 car and buy that new $17,000 car.

Let's visit all of the benefits of scenario two. First of all, there is no risk. If something happens and you can't put back the $321 for a month or two, it is no big deal. No one is calling you or threatening to take your car. Also, you get to move up in car every year. This gives you a chance to decide what you like and with technology changing as quickly as it is, your car won't become obsolete while you are still paying for it. You also will own your car at all times. No one can ever take it away from you. With scenario two, you could get a newer car every year, if you wanted, because you wouldn't have to worry about the payoff versus the value. And of course, there is always the fact that you paid $2,658 less for the car than in scenario one. Many times you can also get a discount when you pay with cash so the amount you paid extra may, in fact, be higher. Just remember, with great discipline, you can receive more pleasure and less pain.

Another common problem is the entitlement attitude we talked about in a previous chapter. We believe that we are entitled to things now and that we shouldn't have to wait for them. Debt has become an easy way out for us and a crutch for us to lean on. You don't have the money to go on vacation right now; no problem, just lean on a credit card to help you pay for it. You don't have the cash to go to college right now; no problem, just use student loans to help you. Debt makes it easy to prolong the pain, but ironically, it just brings us bigger pain later.

Debt has also caused us to lose our common sense. If there were no debt available, and you had to pay cash for your education, you would take the time to make a wiser decision. For example, you can get a perfectly good education by starting off at a local community college and then transferring to a state school for the last 2 years. But we are more worried about the social aspects of college than the education. The average person in 2011 graduated with between $25,000 and $30,000 in student loan debt. This same group had a 9.1% unemployment rate. Having a college degree is no guarantee of a job and how can you pay back a debt without a job? Common sense would dictate that we pay cash for school and choose wisely based on the cash we have so that if we don't get a job in our field right away, we can be patient and work at something else in the meantime. But it is so easy to get a student loan that we just do it and we don't think about the future.

Debt makes us desperate. Are you working just to pay your bills or are you working in your passion? In our example above, if you graduated with student loan debt, you become eager to find a job right away. This can make you seem desperate in job interviews and it will cause you to not take your time in choosing the company you want to work for. In many cases, graduates take the first job offered to them because they need the larger income right away. Not having debt gives you a freedom that is worth more than all the money in the world. If you don't have debt and financial obligations, you have more options and you have the time to really think about purchases and large financial decisions. No debt will allow you to have a vocation, not just a j-o-b.

There is no such thing as "good" debt. In Proverbs 22:7, it says that *"The borrower is slave to the lender."* This is true whether you borrow $5.00 or $500,000. The three debts that get labeled as "good" debts the most are education, car loans, and mortgages. We have already seen in the information above why student loan debt is not a "good" debt. The principle is the same for the other two as well. In addition, cars depreciate in value. Therefore, they are not even good investments. Now, while a house can be a good investment, if bought correctly, there is still a lot of risk being taken when taking on a mortgage. You are gambling that the home will appreciate when you go to sell it and as you have seen lately, this is no longer a guarantee. Debt equals risk, plain and simple.

Most people will tell you that you have to have a FICO score (credit score) in order to get anything. This is not true. You need a FICO score only if you are going into debt or are going to continue to use debt. The FICO score is figured out with the following formula:

35% credit payment history

30% amount owed on credit accounts

15% length of your credit history

10% new credit

10% types of credit used

Do you notice a pattern? Every part of this formula is based on credit, i.e. debt. FICO scores are a representation of how you handle your money. If you are debt free, you will have a FICO score of 0. This is just as powerful as a high score, maybe even more so. It shows that you don't have any debt; therefore, you have money.

You can also have an excellent FICO score without ever going into debt. If you have a credit card, use it and pay if off every month, you can maintain an excellent score without ever going into debt. By the way, this is how credit cards were meant to be used. They were originally established for convenience not for debt. Basically, you need to decide whether you can handle a credit card properly or not which will help you decide whether to maintain a high score or a zero score. Your FICO score is basically your financial reputation and either an excellent score or a zero score shows that you know how to handle money and are in a position to obtain wealth.

My teenage daughter, the other day, told me that people don't want to hear that debt is bad. And she was right. But that doesn't change the facts. If you have debt, you are aware of the stress that it can cause. 52% of marriage end in divorce and 80% of those are for financial reasons, mostly debt. Debt causes stress, depression, anger, financial infidelity, and much more. But since that is probably not what you want to hear, let me say this. Debt, in any form, is not wise. It brings with it all of the emotions and risks mentioned before, but it is also throwing money away. You are paying someone else for the convenience of having it today instead of waiting until you can afford it. Start keeping the money that you work so hard for. Let today be the day you begin your journey to wealth.

### *Getting Out of Debt*

When you decide that you have had enough of being a slave (to the lenders) and decide that you are ready to begin your journey to freedom, one of your first steps will be to pay off all of your debts. Remember, your first step is to stop using debt and begin a cash spending system. However, your decision cannot only be to get out of debt but to stay out. In other words, you want to commit to a lifestyle change. Many people, everyday, decide to lose weight. They decide which diet to go on, what type of exercise to do and how much they want to lose. Then, they jump in. But many of them fail. Not because they are failures, but because they made a short term goal and not a lifestyle change. When you lose weight, you want to keep it off, right? Even if you are one of the success stories, once you reach your goal, you may slowly begin to get away from it. And eventually, you could gain the weight back.

It is the same with your finances. You have to decide to make a lifestyle change. It is not just getting out of debt, but changing many other things in your life, such as habits, attitudes, etc, that will help you handle your finances in a prosperous way, always. There are many great get out of debt plans (diets) out there and most of them work, but if you don't change your lifestyle, you will be right back into debt before you can say "boo". As I said earlier, I work with many clients who come to see me in tears and ready to get out of debt. They are stressed and overwhelmed and don't know where to start. I had a client recently who had worked one of the most popular plans for getting out of debt, but they didn't get very far because they were just doing the steps and not making lifestyle changes along the way. Therefore, when an emergency hit, they panicked and went even further into debt and got behind on their bills. I worked with them and got them back on their feet, but they were still unwilling to make the necessary lifestyle changes to become prosperous. One of their goals was to start putting back for retirement, but every extra dollar they got, they spent. They weren't ready.

What I have learned most from my experience, as well as my clients, is that you can't help people until they are really ready to be helped. This means that your first real step for getting out of debt is to decide if you are ready for a lifestyle change. That is what this entire book is about, making those lifestyle changes. As I said earlier, there are a lot of great plans out there, but it is really easy to get started. First, sit down and make a list of all of your debts. In the workbook, you will find a form for this, but you can use a notepad just as well. List who the debt is with, your monthly payment, your remaining balance, and an estimated time of payoff. You should be able to do this for most of your debts since most credit card companies now list how long it will take to pay off the balance if you pay the minimum. Make sure you are truthful and list every debt. Denial will not help you.

You want to make sure you stay caught up on all of your minimum payments. If something can't get paid because your monthly bills are more than your income, make sure it is a credit card and not your mortgage. Your necessities (food, mortgage, transportation costs, and utilities) always come first. You need to decide the best order in which to pay off your debts. Most people find that smallest to largest works because you can knock out several debts in a short amount of time. If you decide to start with a larger one because of the payment amount or the interest rate, make sure you are prepared mentally for the fact that it will take longer and don't give up. If you find yourself giving up, switch to a few small ones and then go back. The more committed you are the quicker the debts will get paid off. That is another decision that you have to make. If you put all of the extra money you have every month toward debt, you will get out of debt faster than someone who isn't as willing to sacrifice. You have to write your own story. You know you best, what will work for you and your spouse. But just like losing weight, the more committed you are the quicker you will see your results.

You have taken a huge step in your financial life when you make the decision to stop using debt.  I will say it one more time.  That is the most important step.  For me, my first step was my 6 month emergency fund and then I got out of debt.  That was my decision and it worked for me.  It meant that I had to deal with creditors a little longer, but it gave me the comfort I needed to attack my debt with vigor.  What does your story look like?

> *"Every choice you make has an end result."*
> *Zig Ziglar*

# E is for Excuses and Expectations

$\mathcal{D}$o any of these sound familiar?

- ❖ I'm too old, young, or broke to save money.
- ❖ I deserve it.
- ❖ I did it to improve my credit score.
- ❖ My debt is "good debt".
- ❖ The "Little Man" can't get ahead.
- ❖ I can write off the interest on my taxes.
- ❖ I don't need retirement.  I will have Social Security.
- ❖ When I win the lottery, then I'll get out of debt and be ok.

These are just a few of the excuses we use daily to continue in our comfortable, yet very uncomfortable, financial situations.  Here is why these are just excuses.

- You are never too anything to save money, even if it is $5.00.

- If we were truthful with ourselves, we don't really deserve anything, but God wants to bless us. However, He will only bless us in a way that is good for us.

- As we covered in the previous chapter, you can have a credit score of zero or an excellent credit score without ever actually going into debt.

- We also covered "good debt" in the previous chapter and established that no debt is good.

- The "Little Man" can't get ahead, so don't be the "Little Man". Be you, someone who doesn't rely on other people to solve their problems.

- We will cover writing off interest in another chapter, but think about this. Does it make sense to send the bank $10,000 a year to keep from sending the IRS $2,500? Because that is the math.

- I think Social Security speaks for itself. Consider it a miracle and a bonus if you get Social Security when you reach retirement age. In the meantime, don't rely on the government; count on yourself.

- If you do not change how you handle your money, the lottery will only make the problem worse. It will

not fix the problem.  Money doesn't change people.
It only exaggerates what is already there.

An excuse is simply a reason to keep doing what you're
doing.  We use excuses to justify our decisions.  But a
great lesson that I learned is that if you are making a wise
decision, you don't need to justify it.  An example that
happened to me early on in my lifestyle change involved
my washing machine.  My washing machine had died and
I needed to get a new one.  This was an emergency and at
the time I had about $1000 in my emergency fund.  All I
needed was a simple washing machine with regular
cycles, nothing fancy.  So we went washing machine
shopping.  While shopping, I saw the new front load
washing machines and in the color of my laundry room.  I
really wanted it because of the style and the color.  The
price of this washing machine was around $850 and
would take most of my emergency fund.  We had also
seen a simple washing machine, just like we had, at a
local store for $350.  That night, while we were discussing
which washing machine to get, I began justifying why I
"needed" the front load washer and why I should get that
one now instead of the one we could afford and then save
for the one I "wanted" later.  As I was standing in my
kitchen talking on the phone to a friend about my

washing machine dilemma, it hit me. If I had the money, buying the washer I wanted wouldn't matter and I wouldn't have to justify the purchase to anyone, including myself. I immediately went and bought the regular washing machine.

When things like this happen to me, I usually end up thinking back to my parents or other family members who have been wise with their finances. After my washing machine decision, I began to think back and realized that I had never once heard my mom or dad justify or defend a purchase they made. When I was just out of college, my mom bought a Cadillac. I found out later that she had always wanted one and when my parents had saved the money and felt comfortable, they bought her one. At the time that they bought it, she was 53 years old, had worked for 35 years and sacrificed for those 35 years. But all many people could see was the Cadillac. So some people commented. But not once, to anyone, did my mom ever justify their purchase. She didn't have to. They had the money, they were debt free, and they owned their home. Why shouldn't she have a Cadillac?

I could write a whole book just on the excuses we use to stay in the financial condition we are in. But these excuses aren't real and are just getting in the way of your financial freedom. We have to stop making excuses and start believing in what is real. What excuses are holding you back?

## The Blame Game

We talked in the first chapter about the Israelites and how their attitude caused their 11 day journey to take 40 years. But it wasn't just their attitude that caused them hardship. It was also their excuses. They had an excuse for everything. Their biggest excuse was blame. It was always somebody else's fault, never theirs. We always blame somebody else for our financial situations; the government, our employer, the banks, the credit card companies, our parents, and on and on. But I am going to be brutally honest. You are where you are today because of you. That was a hard one for me. But when I owned it, I also realized I could change it. I decided I didn't want my journey to be 40 years of going around the same mountain. I wanted to do what I needed to do, get to the other side as soon as possible and live in the Promised Land.

A colleague of mine was working with a couple where the wife was spending so much on herself (clothes, hair, beauty) that the family had credit card debt over $100,000 and the kids didn't have health or dental insurance. The husband's income was the only income. The husband was oblivious to the finances and how bad they were. It would have been easy to blame the wife for everything and take the finances away from her, but the husband wasn't off the hook. Had they been doing the finances together and he was paying attention, it wouldn't have gotten so out of hand. He just went off to work everyday and left everything to her. She had to own her part, which was easy because it was so obvious, but the husband had to own his part too. If all they did was sit and blame each other and point out where the other went wrong, they would never solve the ultimate problem. The only way for them to fix their finances and move ahead was to stop blaming each other and work together.

I have heard, more than I care too, over the last few years how the credit card companies are to blame for people getting behind in their bills and not being able to pay all of their bills. They are being blamed mostly because they are raising people's interest rates to over 30% with one late payment. But let's look at the painful truth. Their contracts with the consumer state that they have the right to raise your rates when you are late on their account or any of your other accounts. If you have a card with them, you signed this contract, whether you realize it or not. Therefore, you cannot blame them when they raise your rates. Most people want credit cards so bad that they never read the fine print. You should have read the entire contract before you signed it, and when you saw the part about raising your rate, you should have chosen to not get that card.

They say the truth hurts and it does. It is very hard to look at ourselves and see where we went wrong. It was probably one of the hardest steps I had to take, but it was the most important. I am responsible for me. I can choose to use debt or not. I can choose who I do business with and who I don't. I can say "I am done with debt" and be done not matter what other people think. The main reason we blame other people is because we know we are wrong. We don't use blame when we are right. My parents never blamed anyone for their financial situation because they were in good financial shape. When I catch my daughter doing something I told her not to do, she tends to blames everyone else. When she gets a bad grade, it is usually the teacher's fault. We have to start owning our mistakes. Mistakes are huge learning tools. Mistakes can be good if we learn from them and make the changes necessary to not make that mistake again.

Blaming goes back to day one. When God approached Adam and Eve in the Garden, Adam blamed Eve for making him eat the apple and Eve blamed the serpent for tricking her. Adam knew it was wrong and could have said no, same with Eve. But they made their choice. They gave into the temptation of greed and made a mistake. But instead of owning up to it, they blamed. This was the beginning of the real world.

I want to encourage you to stop playing the blame game. Start being truthful with yourself and own your mistakes. Once you identify a mistake, decide what you can do to change it so it doesn't happen again. Remember, you are the author of your story. Write it the way you want it to be and then go and make it happen.

### *Expect the Unexpected*

What are some of your expectations in life? Do you
expect to always have debt? Do you expect to always
have the same job or same type of job? Do you expect to
always stay married? Life doesn't always go the way we
expect it, both good and bad. Many of us set our
expectations low so we are never disappointed. Some of
us set our expectations high so we are almost always
disappointed. You need to have realistic expectations and
sometimes you need to expect the unexpected. Have a
dream and go for it. Set a goal and reach it.

Many people today are angry. I see it every time I drive
on the road, every time I am in a store, and sometimes
even when I am in church. I see it when I counsel
couples. The main cause of anger is that our
expectations of a person or a situation are too high. We
get frustrated when the person or situation didn't meet
our expectations and that turns into anger. But many
times our expectations aren't realistic. And sometimes
our expectation is that our way is the only way and that
is definitely not realistic.

Let's see if we can change some of our expectations. For example, if your expectation is that you will always be in debt, you can change that. You know, by now, that you don't have to stay in debt. It is your choice whether you have debt or not. So you can change your expectation from always being in debt to getting out of debt and never going back. That is a realistic expectation. However, it is not a realistic expectation to believe that you are going to be out of debt right away. It will take time and sacrifice. It is great to set an expectation of when you will be out of debt, but make it realistic. Look at your situation, and then set a realistic expectation.

High expectations not only cause anger but also disappointment. We are going to have disappointments in our life, but if we have realistic expectations, the disappointments will be less painful. If I expect my husband to take out the trash every week, I will be disappointed when he doesn't. But if I have a realistic expectation that he is human and may forget sometimes, then I can let it go when he forgets. With a realistic expectation, I am neither angry nor disappointed when he forgets to take out the trash.

A big problem right now is rising expectations. We expect everybody to do everything for us and the way we want it. We expect to have everything right now exactly the way we want it. And if we don't get it, we literally throw a fit. One day, recently, I was driving and a lady wanted to pull out of a parking lot. I wasn't able to let her out and she flipped me off. She was in her seventies and had a cross hanging around her rearview mirror. She expected me to let her out, no matter what, and she threw a fit when I didn't even though I couldn't. I see this everyday. Her actions made me sad as a person and as a Christian. Debt is the highest it has ever been and a large reason is because of our rising expectations. We want the best house, the best car, the best clothes, and the best education, whether we can afford it or not. And we want it now.

I want you to have dreams and passions and I want you to have everything your heart desires. But I want you to get there with realistic expectations. I want you to enjoy the journey but not be angry and disappointed everyday of it. I hope that today you will decide to stop making excuses and begin to make realistic expectations. When you do this, it will improve your finances, your marriage, your relationships, and your life.

> *"When you make excuses, you deny yourself the opportunity to grow."* Tayo Adeyemi

# F is for Financial Checkups

$\mathcal{E}$ very year you make sure that you and your kids get a yearly checkup at the doctor. Twice a year you make sure that you and your kids see a dentist. It is just as important that you make sure that your finances get a checkup, at least twice a year. The reason that you go to the dentist or the doctor for these checkups is to make sure that everything is okay and if there is a problem, you address it right away before it gets worse. This is the same reason you need to perform a financial checkup. Some people never look at their finances. This can cause you to not have enough insurance, pay too much in fees and not be ready for the future. And if you go long enough without these checkups, you can end up in a situation that will cost you more and may be too late to fix.

In this chapter, we are going to cover some of the more important and money saving areas, which you need to make sure you include in your bi-yearly checkups. But as always, you may have some additional areas that require your attention. Make sure you design your financial checkup for your personal situation. Now, let's dive right in.

### Banking

Many of us open a checking or savings account at a bank and that is the end of it. But that is never the end. First of all, let me say that I believe very strongly in banking at a community, local or credit union level. The big banks have become very greedy over the years and keep getting bought out and changing names and policies. I have had a lot of success banking at a local bank and I personally will never go back to a big bank.

The first thing you need to look at in beginning your banking financial checkup is your monthly bank fees. What are you being charged per month and why? I would not pay more than $2 to $3 per month to have a checking account. If you are paying more than this, shop around. If you find a lower rate somewhere else, but really don't want to change banks, take the lower rate to your current bank and see if they can match it, in writing. Many local banks offer free checking with a $100 minimum balance. This is worth doing in order to save the fees.

Next, look at your transaction fees. What does your bank charge for using their ATM or someone else's ATM? And here is a new one to look out for. Bank of America, about six months ago, tried a flat $5 fee to everyone who had a debit card, whether you used it or not. They did eventually withdraw this fee due to the outcry of its customers. But who's to say they won't try it again, or something similar? Always be aware of everything the bank is charging you. I bank at a local bank that has branches on the East coast. I do not have any fees per month for any of my four accounts. I only have a fee if I use another ATM, but I plan my cash and withdrawals accordingly. Therefore, through diligence and paying attention, I have $0 bank fees per month. So it can be done. Now you may be saying, why go to so much trouble for $3 per month? But it is the little things that will get you. In my case, I am saving $144 per year in bank fees. And it is also the mind set. Why pay even $1 that is not necessary? This mind set is how people become millionaires because they stop giving their money away to banks and corporations.

The last item to address regarding your banking is overdraft protection. They changed the banking policy a little while back that everyone would have overdraft protection unless you told them you didn't want it. Many people didn't cancel it because they didn't know or they thought it didn't matter. Let me take a moment to explain how overdraft works and what will happen if you don't have it. Overdraft protection has one purpose. It is a service that is available to you in the event that you want to spend more money than you have. And with this service comes a fee, usually around $35 per transaction, that you are charged for every transaction that you make without the money to cover it. The purpose of this overdraft protection is to keep you from hearing the word NO. If you try to make a purchase and you don't have the money, the purchase will go through and you will pay $35 in addition to the transaction cost. However, if you do not have overdraft protection and you try to make the same purchase, you will hear the word NO. I have seen people who have paid $43 for a value meal at McDonalds. I have also had clients who were so overdrafted that their entire paychecks went to cover their fees and they could never get ahead. Let me also give you a little inside banking tip. The bank will run the transactions in the order that they can get the most fees out of you. For example, you may have 10 transactions in a weekend and you think only the last transaction will be charged the fee. Then come Tuesday morning, you find out that 3, 4, 5, or even more transactions were charged the fee.

Again, this is a large waste of money. You are giving the bank your hard earned money just because you can't wait until you have the money to make a purchase or because you don't take the time to pay attention. Even if you have only one a month, that is $420 per year you are just handing to the bank. If you have overdraft protection now, you need to go in and cancel it immediately on all of your accounts. This will be very hard for you if you have been using it. But if you are using it, you have allowed it to become a crutch for you and an excuse to not get your finances in order. You work very hard for your money and, as we have discussed before, you should keep what you have earned. Don't give it away to banks and other financial institutions.

### *Insurance*

Today, there are many types of insurance available to us. But, as in many other areas, we have to be aware of what is necessary and what is considered gimmick insurance.

First, let's talk about what is necessary and what every person should have. If you don't have these insurances, at the very least, you should find a way to obtain them and I will discuss inexpensive ways to do just that.

❖ **Health Insurance** – Everyone should have health insurance of some kind and this has been a major debate in this country for quite awhile. I, myself, wasn't able to have health insurance for several years but it was mostly because of my financial situation. But it was by the grace of God that nothing happened to me because at anytime I could have had a health situation that could have financially crippled me for life. Having been there, I am advising everyone to get some form of health insurance, if only for the big stuff. If it is offered through your job, make sure you take advantage of it. If it is not or if you are self employed, there are plans available to you. If you cannot yet afford the plans that cover everything, then get a plan with a HSA or a high deductible. Most of these plans won't cover the first $2500 to $5000 but they will usually cover 100% above that. I would much rather owe $5000 than $100,000. These plans are usually inexpensive and affordable. Make sure you shop around. The best place is an independent insurance agent because they can shop many companies and find the best rates. Many states also offer guaranteed health insurance. These plans are for people with pre-existing conditions who have trouble getting health insurance. They are more expensive, but are still cheaper than paying cash. Many people believe that health insurance is optional until they need it, but then it is too late. You need to make sure that if you don't have health insurance, you find a plan you can afford as soon as possible. And if you have your own insurance and are not covered through your job, make sure you keep shopping it every 6 months to a year. You want to always get the best coverage for your money.

❖ **Life Insurance** – Life insurance is just as important to have as health insurance. If you or your spouse passes away, there is a loss of income that cannot be ignored. Even if you or your spouse is a stay-at-home parent, there would be the cost of hiring someone to do what they do. But just as important as having life insurance is, having the right type is more important. There are two main types of life insurance: whole and term. You should always purchase term life insurance when you can, never whole life insurance and I want to take the time to explain why.

- o **Whole Life Insurance** – Whole life insurance works like this. You buy a policy worth, let's say, $250,000. You will pay, on average, around $250 per month for this coverage. This policy pays the same upon death as a term life policy does. The only difference is that most whole life policies have a cash value which is like a savings account you can borrow against. However, when you die, your beneficiaries do not receive the extra cash value of the plan. They would simply get $250,000. And, if you have borrowed against the policy, and die before it is paid back, the amount you owe would be deducted from the $250,000.

- o **Term Life Insurance** – Term life insurance will cost about $20 per month for $500,000 up to $1,000,000 in coverage, based on your age and your health. So for around 90% less per month in premium, you would receive, at least, double the amount in coverage. Now, if you wanted, you could invest the $230 difference per month into a good growth stock mutual fund and when you die, you would have around $300,000 more that your beneficiary would inherit as well because it is your money.

As you can see from the explanations above, term is almost always better. The only time I would recommend keeping a whole life policy is if you cannot get new term life insurance due to a health condition. Some insurance is definitely better than no insurance at all. Also, always make sure that you keep your current insurance policy until you get a new one in place. You don't want to be without life insurance. And, as in any types of insurance, use an independent insurance broker to insure that you get the best deals out there.

The last question is how much life insurance to have and at what terms. You want to carry about 10 times what your salary is on you. If you or your spouse doesn't have a salary, you would want to carry about $400,000 on them, which is 10 times what it would cost to pay someone else to do what they do. For example, if you or your spouse is a stay-at-home parent and they pass away, you would need to put your kids in daycare and you would probably need help with cleaning and house maintenance. Everyone has a financial value even if they don't bring home a paycheck.

Your terms should be anywhere from 15-25 years, depending on when your kids will be out of college and on their own and when your mortgage will be paid off. If you have no mortgage and no kids to support financially and have hopefully invested well, there is no financial need for life insurance. It then becomes a matter of choice. I know millionaires who have life insurance policies because of the security it gives to the spouse. At that time, do what you want, but in the meantime, get life insurance. It is a necessity.

❖ **Auto Insurance** – Auto insurance is mandatory if you own a vehicle. But you want to make sure you get the most bang for your buck. I will repeat myself and say to always shop around, preferably using an independent insurance agent because they can shop all companies. One of the items that makes your premium higher is the amount of deductible you have. If you have an emergency fund of at least $1000, your deductible should be $1000. Accidents don't happen everyday and if you are a careful driver, you can save a lot of money by raising your deductible to $1000. It is a scary step, but well worth taking if you are ready. I raised my deductible many years ago when I had reached $1000 in my emergency fund. And in as many years, I have only had to pay it once. However, in those years, I have saved $1000's in premiums.

Shopping around and raising your deductible are the two best ways to save money on auto insurance. But make sure you don't cut too many corners. I want to take a moment to warn you of something that I have seen twice in my lifetime. Most agents will tell you to drop collision insurance if you have an older vehicle. The reason for this is because, on an older car, if you total it and it is your fault, the car isn't worth replacing. However, if you do not have the money to replace your vehicle, make sure you have collision insurance. This happened very recently to someone close to me. He owned a car that he paid around $5000 for when he bought it (it was around 8 years old). Because it was an older vehicle, the insurance company told him he didn't need collision insurance and he wanted to save money, so he agreed. Six months later, he was in an accident that was his fault and totaled the vehicle. He didn't have enough in savings at that time to buy another car. If he would have kept the collision coverage, because of his financial situation, the insurance company would have given him a check for what the car was worth and he would have been able to buy another car. So, if you do not have the money to cover the cost of another car in case of an accident, make sure you keep collision coverage. As with all insurances, you don't want too much, but you always want enough.

I have tried to cover in as much detail as I can what I believe to be the three most important insurances to have. Of course, if you have a home, you must have home owners insurance as well or renters insurance if you rent. You should also have long term disability insurance, either through your job or a private company. And lastly, if you are 60 years old or older, you should get long term care insurance, if you are eligible. Your entire nest egg, no matter how large, can be wiped out from nursing home stays alone.

Most insurances beyond these are what we call gimmick insurances. They are valid insurances and will pay if there is a claim, but they are unnecessary and are not cost beneficial. An example of this is cancer insurance. If you have health insurance, you don't need cancer insurance. Another example might be pet insurance. If you are going to own a pet, make sure you have the money to take care of the pet. As I said, these are legitimate types of insurance, but are a waste of money. Always be prepared with the proper types of insurance and the proper coverage and you will be just fine. Don't buy more than you need.

### *Legacy Papers*

We will talk in a future chapter, in great detail, about your legacy. But for now, I just want to mention the importance of doing a financial checkup on your legacy papers. These papers include your will, power of attorney, living trust, etc. At the very least, when you are doing your financial checkups, make sure that these documents are up-to-date and in the proper place, should they be needed. If a major change happens in between checkups, such as a marriage or birth, make sure you change them immediately. You want to make sure your wishes are always known and carried out.

### Debt

We talked about in a previous chapter the importance of knowing how much debt you have and to whom it is owed. If you are in the process of getting out of debt, I would update these balances on a monthly basis. However, if you just have a small amount of debt and are choosing to continue with the payment plans you are currently on, make sure you update the information during your financial checkup so that you can see how much is left on the balances. One of the purposes of the financial checkup is to know your true current financial situation. And hopefully, in looking at your situation, you will decide to pay off some of your debt early.

## *Retirement*

You should receive an investment statement at least every quarter. This statement will show you how your investments are doing. If you see, during your financial checkups, that you no longer feel comfortable with a fund, you will want to talk to your financial advisor to see what is the best move to make. Make sure always use an investment advisor that you feel comfortable with and who is not trying to sell you something. Always make sure you understand what is being taught and that your advisor is a teacher, not a salesperson. If not, take this time, during your checkups or before, to shop around and find someone who has your best interest at heart. Never do an initial investment and then never pay attention to it again. How you manage your retirement funds and investments will decide your financial future. Choose wisely and knowledge, as always, is power. If you don't understand it, don't invest in it.

## *Taxes*

I asked my 13 year old daughter the other day, "When you get a large tax refund, do you know whose money it is and where it comes from?" Even she knew it was your money, not a gift from the IRS. When you receive a large refund check every year, you are simply using the IRS as a savings account with 0% interest. For example, if you are getting back $4800 every year, that means you are having $400 too much taken out of your check every month. What could you do with an extra $400 per month? For many of you, that $400 would change everything in your monthly financial situation. Yet, we continue to give the IRS too much money and then, when we do get our refund checks, we act as if we got a bonus and go and spend it. If you are consistently getting a large refund every year, you need to change your W-4 with your employer. If you go to the IRS website, www.irs.gov, they have a withholding calculator and once you put in your information, they will calculate, within $25, how much you need to have taken out and what you need to claim on your W-4. You are allowed to claim whatever you want. You do not have to claim your actual circumstances. For example, if you are married with three children and the withholding calculator says you need to claim married with one child to break even, you need to change your W-4 to married with one child. This will give you, in our example above, $400 extra every month and in April, when you do your taxes, you will owe nothing.

You need to look at this every year and make sure nothing has changed and there wasn't something odd about this year. An example might be if you bought your first home in 2010, there was an $8000 tax credit. This would not require a change in your W-4 because it was a one time deal. This is an important area to make sure to include in your financial checkup. You never want to owe the IRS, but you don't want to pay them too much and wait up to a year to get it back from them at 0% interest.

## *Miscellaneous*

Lastly, you want to make sure you are always finding the best deals on your miscellaneous bills, such as cable, phone, cell phones, etc. You want to always look at your bills closely and check that there are no extra charges. When you change a plan, double check that there are no penalty charges and write down exactly what the new charges will be. Don't be afraid to change companies if you can get a better deal. It is also okay to try to get your current company to match a deal you found somewhere else, but if they say yes, be sure to get the details of the deal in writing. Remember, always shop around and only get what you need or want. All the little things can add up to big things before long. For example, your teenager doesn't need the most expensive cell phone plan available. They need a way to communicate and maybe, if we're feeling generous, unlimited texting. That is it. If you already have a family plan, this should be around $15-20 per month extra. And as a side note, it is also okay for them to pay for this charge, if they are old enough to have a job.

If you get a financial checkup every six months, you will stay healthy in the area of personal finances. You have to pay attention and always be searching for a way to save money. You won't have money if you keep giving it away. This is the best way to keep your money and let it work for you instead of you working for it.

# G is for Guardrails

*W*hether you want to or not, you must have boundaries in your life. Some of you have very clear boundaries in all areas, some are clear in a few areas, and some of you have no boundaries at all. I had to set up boundaries very early in my lifestyle change because I had had very little in the past. As I was trying to figure out where to talk about boundaries in this book, I heard a wonderful speaker who helped me figure it out. Andy Stanley is a great pastor and motivational speaker and he did a series a little while back called "Guardrails" and in it he gave the perfect analogy for setting up boundaries in your life, not only in your finances, but every area.

A guardrail is a system designed to keep vehicles from straying into dangerous or off limit areas. The guardrail is put in place, not in the danger zone, but before the danger zone. This is so that when you begin to drift toward the danger zone, you will first hit the guardrail, causing only minor damage that can be repaired. If the guardrail wasn't there, there would be nothing to warn you that you are getting close to a danger zone and before you could blink, you would be in the danger zone. Many times the danger zone is a place that can hurt you beyond repair.

The guardrail has one purpose – to save your life. The guardrails and boundaries that you need to set up in your own life have the same purpose. If you look back, you will find that the greatest regrets in your life could have been avoided with a guardrail. People don't regret having guardrails, once they establish them, but they definitely regret not having one when they realize they needed one. In your personal life, a guardrail can be defined as a personal standard of behavior that becomes a matter of conscience. Everyone's guardrails will be different. We will be discussing some areas for having guardrails and I will make some suggestions to get you started, but your boundaries must be your own. Just like personal finance is personal and not cookie cutter, so are boundaries.

Before we go any further, I need you to understand the role that culture, society and your friends and family play in your guardrail system. Society spends all of their time, money and efforts baiting you in certain areas. But when you accept their bait, they judge you for it. A great example of this is in the area of money. Everywhere you turn there are ads and people, even friends and family, challenging you to go into debt. But where are these people after you take their advice and end up with more debt than you can pay? Where are these people when you lose your home because you bought a home before you were ready? This is why you need to establish your own guardrails in your life and don't allow anyone to move your guardrails into a danger zone. You are the one who has to suffer the consequences of your actions. Therefore, you need to set your own personal standards and stick to them, no matter what other people think.

None of us plan to mess up our financial lives, just like none of us plan on running off the road and down an embankment. But in life, the one thing you can expect is the unexpected. Therefore, you need to be prepared with guardrails, just like the traffic planning people prepared a guardrail for you, so that you wouldn't go down the embankment. As I said before, the guardrails have to be yours and yours alone. But I am going to talk to you about a few specific areas in personal finance and give you some suggestions for guardrails that have worked very well for me. When you finish reading each section, make sure to stop and take time to make some guardrails for yourself, either using the workbook or a piece of paper. In the beginning, you need to write them down and go over them daily. After a short while, they will become part of your conscience and you won't need the list. It will become your lifestyle.

### *Debt*

Debt is the biggest area where we need a guardrail and the one where we most likely do not have one. I have always taught, from the beginning, that your income is your boundary. When you spend beyond your income, which is money you don't have, you are in the danger zone. But the guardrail for debt needs to be more than just your income because even if you spend all of your income, you will not have any savings or retirement. The guardrail that I suggest with spending is no more than 80% of your income. This allows 10% for saving and 10% for giving. This is a minimum. The lower your spending percentage is the wealthier you will become.

We dedicated a whole chapter to debt and the risk it entails, as well as what a life full of debt looks like. My guardrail in this area is plain and very simple. I will not have debt or use debt to purchase anything. If I don't have the money, I don't buy it, whatever it is. Now, there are people, like my parents, who have had one or two credit cards their whole life and have always paid the balance off every month because for them, they are a convenience. They never spend more than they have. They just use them instead of debit cards because debit cards are unfamiliar to them. In those cases, their guardrail is different, but still exists. You have to decide what your guardrail is going to be. But let me offer you a warning that I had to heed. If you have used debt for most of your life, and it has gotten you in way over your head, your guardrail needs to be no debt. The key to finding the best guardrail for you is to be honest with yourself about where your danger zone is. If you use debt for everything, debt is your danger zone because using it causes you to overspend and not be able to save and give. I set my guardrail at no debt many years ago when I filed for bankruptcy and started my financial life over. I wasn't going back to that life again. There was nothing but stress and unhappiness and I wanted more for myself than that. But I had to have a come to Jesus moment with myself. I couldn't handle debt. I couldn't have a credit card and not use it. I couldn't pay it off every month. I wanted to, the intent was there, but something always prevented me, usually lack of money. I couldn't have a car payment and still save 10% and give 10%. I had to be honest with myself and I realized it didn't make me a bad person. Truthfully, most people don't handle debt well which is why God never says debt is okay anywhere in the Bible. He knew us before we knew ourselves.

I want you to take the time right now to decide your guardrail regarding debt. You have read my perspective on debt. If you are a person of faith, I hope you realize God's perspective on debt. Use your knowledge and truth to develop a guardrail in this area. And once you have it set, follow through no matter what other people think. I can almost promise you they will think you have lost your mind and will laugh at you. But remember what we tell our kids. It doesn't matter what everybody else thinks. You have to stand up for your convictions and don't let anyone tell you different. I haven't ever met anyone who got out of debt and decided to stop using debt that regretted it and wanted to go back.

## *Time*

I know you are saying, "Debbi, what in the world does time have to do with my finances?" It can have a lot to do with your finances. How many activities are your kids involved in? How many nights do you eat out or grab something at a drive-thru because you didn't have time to cook? How much more do you spend every month because you don't have the time to look over your spending and your budget? Are you starting to see how time can affect your finances?

I have many friends and family members that I dread calling to catch up with because I know the first thing I am going to hear is how busy they are. With all of the choices and opportunities available to us, we have become a very "busy" society. This busyness can not only affect our family connections, spiritual connections, and stress us out; it can also affect our money. Here are a few questions you need to answer about you and your family to see how much "busy" is costing you.

1. How much money do you spend in activities in a month?

2. How much money do you spend in gas for these activities in a month?

3. How much money do you spend extra in food on the nights you have these activities?

4. How much family time is lost each month with these activities?

I believe that some of you will find out you are busier than you need to be or can afford. I am not saying that kids should not participate in activities, especially the ones where there is no financial burden. But I have seen too many couples who can't pay their mortgage but have their kids in activities costing $100's every month. You need to set up guardrails on your time and your money in this area. This may mean your child has to do one activity this year and one next year. This may mean they have to choose. But life is full of having to make hard, wise choices. Take the time right now to sit down and look at the cost, both financially and emotionally for all activities, including yours. Then decide what you can do, without stress, and set your guardrails accordingly. It may be painful at first, but I promise, this is a guardrail you won't regret.

## *Spending*

Can you guess what I am going to suggest as your guardrail for spending? You're right. It is the dreaded "b" word, budget. There is a chapter later on about having a budget (spending plan) and how to start and maintain a budget. But it is important, in the meantime, to realize why a budget is important. If you don't have a spending guardrail, i.e. a budget, you are just going to keep spending and never know where your danger zone is until you are in it. A budget becomes your boundary and your guide. Many people see a budget as a prison, keeping them from the freedoms they want. As you will see, you decide what your budget is based on your income and goals. What a budget will bring to light, however, is your reality and that is what scares people the most.

Don't be afraid to do a budget because of what it may tell you. You have to own your truth, however frightening it may be. And when you know your truth, you can set up your budget (guardrail) in a way that will keep you safe and out of the danger zone.

If you do not have any debt, you may find a budget unnecessary. However, a tool that is great for everyone, even in addition to a budget, is a spending log. This can be done on a computer, but also can be done very easily on a piece of paper. You need to know how you are spending your money and be able to look at areas that need to decrease or increase. Doing this can cause you to have more wealth. Do not think that just because you have money, you don't need to know where your money is going. Your income is your greatest wealth building tool and if you aren't sure where it is going, you can't know your wealth potential. This is also an excellent tool for couples. It is a great way to communicate and gives both parties access to where the money is going at all times. This allows for accountability not blame.

Take the time right now to do a preliminary budget and see what your guardrails look like. Your spending plan can be tweaked once you get to the spending plan chapter, but start now to begin establishing your guardrails. Also, start tracking your spending. This will also aid you in establishing the best guardrails in this area.

### The Secret

I am getting ready to give you the secret to everything financial. This secret is priceless and if you do this one thing, you will be in a great position financially. Now, if you are a late starter and made some financial mistakes, as I did, you may have to tweak this secret just a little. Are you ready?

The secret to financial freedom is very simple. Out of every penny you make or obtain, give 10%, save 10% and live on 80% or less. That is the secret. If you do nothing else, but this one thing, you will have wealth and financial freedom. Now, as I said, if you are late to the game, you will have to bump up your 10% savings in order to have a good nest egg come retirement, but you can do this. First and foremost, you must give. If you are not a giver, you will become greedy with your money. You will begin to live under the assumption that it is all for your consumption and no one else can have any. As a person of faith, I always give at least 10%. I know that, even though all of it is God's, he only asks for 10% to be given back to Him and so I give before I do anything else. You can give to your local church, if you are a member somewhere, or to a ministry, or you can even give to help the needy and troubled. However it looks in your world, make sure you are a giver.

Now once you have given, then you should save next, at least 10%. Remember, the more you save, the more you will have. This secret is the minimum required for financial freedom. And last, you need to learn to live on what is left. I know many couples who have set their spending at 70% or even lower in order to have more saved and be able to give more when they see a need. This secret needs to be taught to every teenager and young person in this country. If they can do this one thing, and learn to live on 80% of their income, no matter what the amount, they will always have financial freedom in their lives.

Take time now to set your guardrails using this secret formula. Decide how much of your income you are going to give, save and spend, keeping in mind that 10-10-80 is a minimum. Once you set your percentage for your household, you can then begin to implement them into your spending plan and future financial goals.

I have given you just a few of the guardrails I believe to be essential in personal finance. I hope as you have taken the time to set these guardrails for your household that you have thought of more areas where you need guardrails. Remember, personal finance is 90% emotion and 10% math. This means that you will probably need a lot more emotional guardrails set in order to accomplish the financial ones. Guardrails are very important. If you have run off the road already with your finances, know that today is the day to get back on the road to recovery and set your financial life on the right course. And this time, you will be able to avoid the danger zone, thanks to your new guardrails.

# H is for Habits

*A* habit is defined as an acquired behavior pattern regularly followed until it has become almost involuntary. Two things are important in this definition. One is that a habit, both good and bad, is an acquired behavior. That means that you are not born with habits. They are actions that you have tried and chosen to keep. The second is that they become almost involuntary. This means that most of the habits that you have, again both good and bad, you may not even know you have them. One of the exercises in the workbook, if you are following along, is to make a list of your good habits and make a list of your bad habits. How hard is this for you? The first time I did this, it was very challenging. On the one hand you don't want to believe that some of your habits are bad. And on the other hand, most people can't recognize the good in themselves. But you need to be able to identify your habits, especially the bad ones, in ordered to modify them in a positive way.

The main thing I want to accomplish with this chapter is to identify habits that may be hurting you financially and to also help you with habits that can help you financially. Habits are not just physical, they are also emotional. If you can recognize and identify the habits in your life, it will become easier with time to replace the bad with good.

I hear too many times "That is just the way I am" or "That is just the way I was raised." You may have formed a habit based on how you were raised and you may have kept the habit because you believe that you can't change certain things, but both of these are myths. No matter how you were raised, you get to write your own story. You don't have to become the circumstances in which you were raised.

I hope as you read this chapter, you will be able to realize the difference in habits and genes. And I hope that I can motivate you to form habits that are good for you, both financially and emotionally. To form a new habit isn't easy, especially if you have had an old habit for a very long time. But it is definitely worth it. And I can say that with certainty because I have lived it. To form a new habit takes between 21 and 30 days. But you have to change it on purpose. Changing habits is not magic. You can't say one day "I want to stop using credit cards" and you magically never use them again. You have to take steps every day to form a new habit of paying with debit or cash. I will not lie to you. It will be very hard at first. But every time, it will get easier and easier until one day you will have formed a new habit.

### *Jump Right In*

We are just going to dive right in right away. They say the best way to pull off a band aid is quickly so it is less painful. Realizing your bad habits and standing in your truth about them is going to be very painful. But I want to jump right in and address these habits first because they are the hardest and the most costly.

Let me ask you a question and I need you to be honest. Do you have an addiction? Think before you answer. Now, if you said no, I want you to think really hard if there is anything you do over and over that makes you feel better. There are the obvious additions, such as drugs, alcohol, and tobacco and there are the not so obvious ones of shopping, food and money. Most people who have them won't admit it because nobody wants to have an addiction. Even if you answered no to my question, please read on. Because even if you don't have an addiction, you do have bad habits. We all do.

I am not here to judge you. As a matter of fact, in my past, I have had a shopping addiction, a money addiction and a food addiction. So I know a little bit about this subject. People with addictions have trouble knowing that is what they have because nobody wants to be addicted or even have a bad habit. When you are trying to identify your bad habits, you will need to ask yourself some really tough questions. For example, do you have a glass of wine everyday or do you go to the mall every week, whether you need anything or not? How do you feel when you don't have a glass of wine or go to the mall? Are you happiest when you have that glass or are in the mall and are you depressed when you don't? These are just examples to get you started. But the toughest part is going to be being truthful about the answers.

Again, I am not trying to judge. What I want to help you realize is how much your addictions and bad habits are costing you financially. I won't even mention what they are costing you relationally or emotionally. I will focus only on the financial part. I am going to list below the average cost per year of the addictions we mentioned a moment ago.

- ❖ One cocktail per day with vodka - $ 1300.00
- ❖ One glass of wine per day - $ 1300.00
- ❖ Smoking one pack per day (one person) - $ 1820.00
- ❖ Shopping once a week at mall - $ 10,400.00
- ❖ Marijuana addiction - $ 6200.00
- ❖ 3 sodas per day - $ 1450.00

Now, as I said before, these are obvious addictions that will cost you financially. But I now want to give you an example of one that may not be as obvious. Have you ever heard of a driving addiction? Probably not because I made it up. I drive many miles across this great country and I have noticed something. Most people drive really fast and very aggressively. And the reason that I know that this is a habit is because I used to be one of those people. I label it an addiction because I think that people don't realize the cost, who they are hurting, and they have no intention of changing. I used to drive about 70 in a 65, which isn't bad, but I would drive 60 in a 40 or 45. I always had to go fast even when I wasn't in a hurry. This is when I realized I had formed a bad habit that needed changing. And as I worked on this change, I realized a very important side advantage. I saved money.

Of course there is the obvious savings – no speeding tickets. The average speeding ticket is $150.00, not to mention the rise in your insurance rates. But I also observed another savings. Did you know that cars are designed to get the optimum gas mileage at 55 miles per hour? When you are driving 75 and 80 miles per hour (and you are because I see you every day), you are using a lot more gas. At the time I am writing this chapter, gas is averaging $3.86/gallon. When I slowed down and obeyed the speed limit, I began to average 50-60 more miles per tank of gas. This was a savings of $ 7.72 per tank. If you use only one tank a week, that is a total savings of $400 per year. If you use more, the savings are more. I also saved money on the maintenance of my vehicle because I wasn't running it crazy. Today, my minivan has 413,000 miles on it. I have saved an additional $25,000 by not having to get a new vehicle at 250,000 miles like most people do.

I know this all seems silly and you are saying, "Debbi, what in the world does this have to do with anything?", but I am trying to show you how bad habits, even the not so obvious ones, can cost you money. Another silly bad habit that could cost you a lot of money is the habit of a negative attitude. A negative attitude is not just about your words and tone, but also about your thinking. Many people have been laid off and lost jobs in the last few years. But how they looked at that lay off or job loss and how they proceeded forward determined their success in finding a new job. If you are negative about the situation and don't believe in yourself or your abilities, it will show in a job interview. If you are bitter about the previous employer and the situation, it will show in a job interview. The biggest reason for someone finding a job within a few months or taking 2 years or more to find a job is not the economy. It most likely is their attitude. Having a negative attitude has financial consequences, as we see in the above example. When you are not open to options and always negative about your current circumstances, you are less likely to fix them. Therefore, you will continue in those circumstances longer than someone with a positive attitude.

There are more bad habits that have financial consequences than I can talk about in this chapter. A good exercise, which is included in the workbook, is to look at your bad habits, honestly, and see if these habits are costing you financially. Remember, bad habits are not just physical but are many times emotional. Make sure to include all of the bad habits you can come up with. This exercise is not to depress you, but quite the opposite. It is to motivate you to your truth and to motivate you to change anything that is getting in the way of your goals and dreams and being the person you want to be.

### *Relax a Little*

Now that I have completely drained you emotionally, I want to relax a little and focus on some good habits. We all have our share of good and bad habits. We also all have our share of good habits that we would like to aspire to. One of the biggest obstacles regarding habits is realizing that everything you do or think is probably a habit. Just this week a friend of mine shared out of a book that she was reading. The author said that 90% of what we do is out of our subconscious or out of habit. And we can never get that completely out of us but we can dilute it. Let me give you an example. A good habit to form when it comes to personal finance is patience. Even though we are all born with patience, it is something that leaves us very quickly. There can be many reasons for this such as the way we are brought up, the people and environment around us and society. Right now in the world of finance it is very easy to not wait for anything. You can get a loan on anything from a car to a car stereo. But as you know, this has its own consequences.

So let's say that waiting to save and buy what you want is not your forte. But you have decided that you want to be prosperous and you have come to realize that patience is a key to that. Therefore, you have decided to form a new habit of patience. Well, unfortunately you can't wave a magic wand and suddenly become patient. Every time you want something, your subconscious is going to say buy it now, no matter what the consequence. So every time you want to buy something and that little voice pops up in your head, you will need to stop and think. You will have to think on purpose and out loud that you need to wait and save to buy that item. You can write the item down, the cost, and how you will save for the item. This will take a lot of practice to form this new habit but it will be well worth it. Patience will save you a lot of money in interest and in buying things you really didn't want. It will also help you to make better choices when you do have the money to buy the items you want or need. This new way of thinking will begin to dilute the bad habit, but the habit will always be there. Even if you are a millionaire, there will be times when you will not want to be patient. But the more you practice the new habit, the smaller the old habit will become.

I want to take a moment and list some of the habits that can either keep you from prosperity (bad) or help you reach all your goals and dreams (good). Take a moment and be honest about which side you fall on in these areas.

### Good vs. Bad

- ❖ Patience vs. Impatience
- ❖ Saver vs. Spender
- ❖ Cash vs. Debt
- ❖ Think vs. Impulse
- ❖ Discipline vs. Undisciplined
- ❖ Wisdom vs. Society
- ❖ Giving vs. Selfish
- ❖ Peace vs. Stress
- ❖ Freedom vs. Pleasing Others
- ❖ Learn from mistakes vs. Keep making same mistakes
- ❖ Humble vs. Haughty

- ❖ Kindness vs. Anger
- ❖ Satisfied vs. Keeping up with the Jones
- ❖ God's ways vs. Man's ways

These are just a few of the habits that we have in our everyday lives. I am here to tell you as a living testimony that bad habits will do nothing but bring you down. Before my bankruptcy, I was probably 90% bad. Not that I was a bad person, but I had formed some very bad habits when it came to my money. But I didn't realize that I could change my habits and my way of thinking. If you only get one thing from this chapter, let it be this. YOU decide your story. YOU control your thinking and YOU can change your thinking as soon as YOU decide to. It doesn't matter about your past or how you grew up. Today is the day for change and YOU are the only one who can change it.

*"The chains of habit are too weak to be felt until they are too strong to be broken."*
*Samuel Johnson*

# I is for Ignorance, Indulgence and Impatience

These words are three of the most important traits that lead to debt and personal financial issues. But how can you know if you have one of these traits if you don't know what they look like and what they mean. You know by now that this book is all about truth. In this chapter, like the others, you are going to have to stand in your truth and be honest about whether or not you carry these traits and then decide whether you want to do something about them. There are some traits we have such as eye color, skin color and height that we cannot change. But there are also traits we have such as hair color, crooked teeth and weight that we can change. Luckily for me and for you, these three traits can be changed and I will show you how. So let's dive right in.

## *Ignorance*

First, I want to define ignorance for you. Ignorance is the lack of knowledge. Stupidity is knowing something is wrong or that a decision is bad and doing it anyway. And both ignorance and stupidity define our actions, not our person. That is the most important point of this chapter. You are not an ignorant person or stupid and I never want you to call yourself that. However, we all have areas of ignorance (because we can't all know everything) and we have all done stupid. I love using examples in my life because I want you to know I understand and have been there. I am not sitting up in the air looking down on you, thinking this is for you and not me. I will tell you right now, I am ignorant when it comes to fixing your car. I have some knowledge of noises and what they mean, having owned so many used cars, but I cannot even begin to fix a car. I am also ignorant when it comes to playing the tuba. I know music but wouldn't even know where to begin with playing the tuba. These are silly examples, and my list is long, but there are areas that I just do not have the knowledge needed to perform the task. But, if I choose to, I can gain knowledge in any area. This is what I did with my finances many years ago.

I was ignorant when it came to money. This shocked many people as I have a BS degree in Accounting. But see, I was taught how to handle money in companies, how to handle money on paper and how to get everything to balance. I wasn't taught the emotions of money and how to make the financial decisions of the companies. That was up to the owners and executives. I just processed the numbers based on their decisions. Personal finance is 90% emotion and 10% math. I was an expert in the 10% math part, but I was very ignorant in the 90% emotion part.

Knowledge is the cure for ignorance, in any area. My problem was I didn't have the proper knowledge. I only had what people told me and showed me through their actions. I've touched on this area already but it is worth repeating. I saw what my mom and dad had. But I didn't have the knowledge of what they had to do to get it. So I just assumed that when I graduated college and got my first job, I would go get what they had. I never knew (at that time) that my mom and dad had always paid cash for cars. I just assumed they had a car loan like everyone else. How else could they ever afford a new car? Paying with cash seemed impossible to me.

My parents were very private when it came to their money, understandably so, which meant the examples of how to handle money were everywhere, but the teaching was missing, the step by step. I was always told to save for stuff, but I couldn't see how. I also believe some of this is generational. When my parents were growing up, they didn't have a lot so it was easier for them to appreciate money as they had more and learn to be wise with it. They could see what saving looked like because it was the only way to get anything. When I began my life journey, debt was an epidemic and used for everything. My example was a society who charged everything and had to have it now.

Unfortunately, my ignorance led to stupidity. I remember one year, I owed taxes to the IRS for about $1200.00. Well, I didn't have $1200.00 so I didn't file. Well, needless to say that $1200 turned into about $2500.00 and many unfriendly letters from the IRS. Doing this didn't make me stupid. But I knew I needed to file my taxes and I chose not to because I didn't have the money. Therefore, my choice was stupid. There was a key element to my stupidity. When I was faced with a bill I couldn't pay, I just ignored it. Just an FYI – debts don't go away, especially the IRS. As most of you know, my problem got bigger than me and I ended up filing for bankruptcy. When this happened, I decided it wasn't going to happen again. And the only way I could prevent it from happening again was knowledge. So I began to study many things: my past mistakes (what had brought me to this point), the Bible, and books written by experts in this area. I learned more from the Bible than anything because I truly believe it is just a book of common sense. The books I read were great, but don't ever do something just because someone says to, even me. If you understand what they are saying and believe it can help you, try it. But be willing to change it again if it isn't working for you. My mistakes have also helped me a great deal. A mistake is only good if we learn from it. I never let my mistakes define me or my future.

I have a confession to make. Sometimes, I still do stupid. There are still times when I know I shouldn't buy something, but I do anyway. But, thank God, it is never anything big. My ignorance has lessened over the years and my stupid has lost many zeros because of the knowledge I obtained. Knowledge is power. It is what has gotten me where I am today. You are not ignorant or stupid. You can gain the knowledge you need to make the right choices, get out of a mess, and be prosperous. Knowledge is everywhere. You just have to go find it.

### Indulgence

Indulgence is a form of greed. To indulge means to give into your desires. I once heard a great definition for greed. "Greed is the assumption that everything is for my consumption." Greed and indulgence both basically mean getting what you want no matter what the cost. All debt is a symptom of indulgence. You couldn't wait to get what you wanted and you assumed that you could have it even if you didn't have the money. Therefore, you borrowed the money to indulge yourself. Indulgence can come in the form of cars and houses or it can also come in the form of purses and golf clubs.

Indulgence is also a form of selfishness. Many items are bought for the sole reason that you wanted it. Nothing more. You didn't care how much it cost, you didn't look at the total cost after interest, you didn't care about 6 months from now when your finances may change and sadly, you probably didn't care how if would effect your spouse or family. You simply bought it because you wanted it. In Luke 14, Jesus tells us wise people always count the cost before doing anything. Indulgence doesn't allow for that. There is also several other keys to prosperity that indulgence doesn't allow for: patience, wisdom, and giving.

I could write an entire book about the indulgences available to us. But I want to talk about one to give you an idea of what an indulgence looks like. One of the best examples of an accepted indulgence in our country today is a college education. Now, before you all send me letters, I believe a college education is great for many people and I cherish mine. But just like every other decision with a financial component, it needs to be thought through and the cost counted. Two thirds of the students attending college for a 4 year degree are doing so on student loans. Many of these students made the decision to go to college, signed up for the loans and never looked back. They didn't think about how they would pay back the loans. They just assumed they would get a loan, go to school, get a job, and pay back the money. However, currently, only 37% of students are able to make their student loan payments. In talking with people all over this country, I have come to a conclusion. A college education is an indulgence. In a future chapter, I will cover more about how to go to college without loans and making sure you go to college for the right reasons. But to attend college, without a serious passion in mind and without the money, is an indulgence. I read an article this week that talked about how young adults aren't the only ones with this issue. Now, there are many older borrowers who will be paying back student loans with their Social Security checks. This stems mostly from going back to school after a job loss or co-signing for children and grandchildren. I truly believe that a college education should be the goal of anyone whose passion requires further education. But as with any decision, we have to count the cost.

I hope that you will take a moment and be honest about the indulgences in your life. Many indulgences are in the past and nothing can be done to correct them. You have to follow through with the consequences. But some indulgences can be corrected. If your indulgence is a car, you can sell it, pay off the debt, and get a car within your cash budget. This can be done with many of your indulgences, including homes, but you first have to admit that is what they are. People believe that indulgences make them look cool. But the reality is they just make you broke. Do you know what is cooler than cool? Having money in the bank, being able to pay your bills every month, and save for an awesome retirement. Now that's cool.

### *Impatience*

Impatience simply means I want it now and I am not going to wait. I am writing a children's book entitled "I Want It and I Want It Now." It would also be a great title for an adult book. You may not think that this applies to you, that you are not impatient, but if you have debt of any kind, you are. Debt is the tool we use to fuel our impatience.

Let's take a trip down memory lane for just a moment. Many years ago, before my time, when you wanted to buy a washing machine, it went something like this. You would go down to the local store and pick out the one you wanted (there were usually only a few to choose from). Then you would tell the owner what you wanted and give him a deposit toward it. You would then go back and keep paying on it until it was paid off. Once it was paid off, they would deliver it and you would have a brand new washing machine. Does anyone know what this is called? This was (and is) known as layaway. And to go one step further, when the washing machine would break, you would call a repair man to fix it. You would keep your washing machine for many, many years until it couldn't be fixed anymore and then you would repeat the process.

Now, let's look at that same scenario today. Your washing machine is working just fine, but you decide you want one of the newer models that is prettier and has more features on it than yours. Your neighbor has one and you just love how it looks. So you look through the sales papers and go to all of the big box stores and find the best deal on the one you want. You go to the register and pay for it using a credit card. And sometimes, if you are lucky, the store is offering 0% financing if you open a new credit card with them. So you decide to add one more card to your collection. Now you have to decide what to do with your perfectly fine washing machine at home, so you decide to sell it to someone who doesn't have a washing machine and is happy to have one that works that they can pay cash for. You get your new washing machine and are so happy with it. Then the bill comes and you find out that the 0% financing is only good for 6 months and you can only make the minimum payments. Therefore, it takes you 5 years to pay off the washing machine and costs you $300 more in interest. 3 years later they come out with a newer model that you just have to have and you start the process all over again, while still paying for the one you have.

Now, I know this last scenario isn't everyone, but it is many people today and I hear stories everyday with this same theme. We used to be a replacement society and now we are an upgrading society. We do not have the patience to wait until what we have is all used up to get the next thing. I decided something this week that falls in this category without realizing it. My minivan is a 2006 with 413,000 miles on it. I like my minivan and I have been the only owner of it. I decided that I am going to keep getting it repaired until it cannot be fixed anymore. I never want a car payment again. And I have my next car in mind (even though it may change with time). I am going to pay cash for that car as well and it will be more than my minivan. So, I have decided to wait patiently and keep saving for my next car. You need to understand something, however. I have to do this on purpose. I am not a superhuman. I am tempted with cars everyday. But I know that this is what is best in order for me to have the financial life I want to have. Who cares what kind of car I am driving when I am sitting on the porch of my lake house (that I don't own yet), sipping sweet tea and enjoying my retirement, at age 65.  I will never fulfill that dream if I am always upgrading and never replacing.

Ignorance, indulgence and impatience will all cause you to not reach your financial goals because every one of them lead to debt.  We will talk a lot about contentment in another chapter, but you have to learn to be content with what you have.  Take your time when buying what you buy, pay only with cash, and only buy what you need or what you save for because you want it bad enough to sacrifice.  Know that you have options.  Grandma always said "There is more than one way to skin a cat."  If you only have two options, you don't have enough information.  Knowledge, moderation, and patience will take you places with your personal finances you never knew were possible.

> *"When we know better, we do better."*
> *Maya Angelou*

# J is for the Joneses

$\mathcal{W}$ho are the Joneses? They are different for everyone. For you, the Joneses may be your neighbor, your co worker, a life long friend, or maybe even a stranger. The Joneses are whoever it is you are trying to become or be better than. If the Joneses get a new Buick, you need to buy a new Lexus. If the Joneses get new living room furniture, you need to redo your entire kitchen. Obviously, you have figured out by now, I am referring to the saying "keeping up with the Joneses." Originally "Keeping Up with the Joneses" was a comic strip. However, over the years, it has become a phrase to describe the philosophy of comparing your standard of living with that of your peers. The Joneses used to be the most wealthy, but in our current consumption based society, the Joneses can be anybody. Most of us have a Joneses, even if we don't know them personally (although odds are you know exactly who your Joneses are).

The American Dream has changed over the years. The American Dream used to be about freedom of religion and freedom from oppression. You reached success through hard work. Today the American Dream is about entitlement. You are entitled to own a house, a car and stuff, whether you have the money or not. Trying to live the American Dream today brings us nothing but stress, overworking, waste and indebtedness. But this doesn't have to be your American Dream.

There are two main causes for the change in the American Dream. One is jealousy and the other is discontentment. If we can find a way to be content with what we have and stop comparing ourselves to everyone else, we can live the true American Dream. I love progress. I am very thankful that I don't have to wash my clothes by hand and hang them out to dry. I am very thankful that I can use my computer to write this book instead of typing it on a typewriter. I am thankful that when my car breaks down, I don't have to wait for a policeman or walk to get help. I can just call from my car. This country has made such great progress in technology and improving how things work over the last 30-40 years and I think that is great. But unfortunately, it has brought about a negative. It has given us a lot of items to choose from and to consume. And it has stepped up the "keeping up with the Joneses" to a whole new level. Every month, it seems, they are coming out with a better cell phone. Every year, the cars have more and more technology. They will even park themselves now. This is our new world we live in. There will always be a "better" to consume. If you don't get your jealousy and discontentment under control, you will spend your whole life (and most of your money) seeking "better."

### *Jealousy*

Jealousy is when you resent someone for having something that you want. Now you may not think you are jealous of someone, but how do you react when that person gets something? I remember when my mom bought her Cadillac, which I have told you about before. There were several people who made snide comments regarding her new car. Now, of course, they said it jokingly, but I believe deep down they were jealous because she had a new luxury car and they didn't. They didn't care how she got it. All they cared about was that she had something that they wanted. Let me ask you a question. Do you know someone who has lost something, a house or a job, and deep down you were happy they lost it? That is jealousy.

Jealousy has helped to change the American Dream because we want what everybody else has. And we will do whatever we need to do to get it. We overwork, we go into debt, and we risk our savings and retirement, all just to have stuff. This year we lost a great business leader, Steve Jobs. He said "Your time is limited. Don't waste it trying to live someone else's life." Jealousy is talked about in the Bible as coveting. Most of us, even if you are not a Bible person or a God person, follow the Ten Commandments as a guideline for living. The tenth commandment says to not covet anything of your neighbors. It barely made the list, but it was important enough to make it. Now, just in case you are not sure who your neighbor is, it is anyone you come in contact with. So if your friend gets a new car, be happy for him. If your sister gets the kitchen of her dreams, be happy for her. It's that simple. Just be happy for them.

Don't allow jealousy to kill your American Dream. Don't allow jealousy to make you overwork, miss out on spending time with your family, and put you in debt that you may never get out of. Your possessions are not as important as your peace. By the way, all of the things you are coveting and buying to "keep up with the

Joneses" you will not be able to take with you. Things have no ability to make you happy.

## *Discontentment*

Jealousy and discontentment are sisters to each other and many times one leads to the other. When you are not content with what you have, you become jealous of what other people have. When I talk about discontentment, I am talking about it in the context of stuff. Would you be able to commit right now to not buying anything that is not a true necessity for one year? Many of us would say no problem until that new gadget comes out or until our neighbor gets that new thing. This is because we are not truly content.

There is one thing that fuels our discontentment. That is awareness. If you never saw a granite countertop, you would be happy with your laminate one. If you never saw a Mercedes, you would be content with your Toyota. It is only when you become aware of what is available that you become discontent with what you have. Discontentment has never been more prevalent than in today's society. As I shared in a previous chapter, I tend to watch the house buying shows on television. And as I have said before, many times they frustrate me. I see young couples walk into an older home and they say it is too small and not updated enough. They often say "Everything will need to be updated." They are discontent with these homes because they are aware there is something different out there. What they usually don't realize is the price tag that comes with it, but that is another matter. Years ago, people were happy with these homes and saw them as a blessing because there weren't many options to choose from. Today the world is filled with bigger and better and most people won't be content until they get it.

What they also don't realize is if that is their attitude, they will never be content because there will always be bigger and better. We must learn to be content where we are. As long as you are always trying to get more, you will never be content. We all have an appetite for stuff. It is hard to exist in a world with so much stuff and not want some. However, your appetite for stuff, just like your appetite for food, will never be satisfied. When we are hungry, we eat. Once we eat, we are satisfied for a short while, but then we become hungry again and we feed our appetite by eating again. This is what most people do about their stuff appetite. But there is a solution. Have you ever been on a fast? If not, this is what happens.

The first day or two you are still really hungry, but you continue to press through the hunger. By day three, your appetite is much less. You have lessened your appetite for food by not feeding it. This is the same with your stuff. It will be really hard at first. You will have stuff pains, just like you have hunger pains. But the longer you don't feed your stuff appetite, the less hungry it is.

In the Bible, Paul said that he had learned to be content no matter what his circumstances. He also told Timothy that contentment is great gain because we brought nothing into this world and we can take nothing out.

Let me ask you a question and you need to be honest. Are you pretending? Is the financial life you are living a visual of your truth or is it an illusion of what you want it to be? Who are you trying to impress? You need to decide today to be content and not be jealous of anyone or anything. I am going to let you in on a little secret, well actually two secrets. The people you are trying to impress and immolate are not going to be there for you when it comes time to pay your bills or when it is time to retire and you can't afford it. Secondly, those same people are probably living their own illusion.

I am not saying that you shouldn't want things and that you shouldn't save to get them. I have things that I have saved for and own. But you need to be content where you are and stop comparing what you have and who you are with everyone else. Lay out your visions and your goals and figure out how to get there and stop worrying about everybody else. Several years ago, I was really into watching "Clean House" on television and the show inspired me to go through my stuff and get rid of stuff I wasn't using. Now, I was not a hoarder and I am thankful to say my house didn't look anything like the houses on television, but I realized I had stuff I wasn't using and never would. It took me 4 yard sales to get rid of all of the stuff I didn't need or wasn't using. In my spending days, or days of discontentment, I would buy something just because of the color whether I could use it or not. When my daughter was little, she loved Arial from the "Little Mermaid" so I would go on spending binges and buy her everything Arial. I had 30 purses that I never used because I didn't like changing purses with my outfits, even though that is why I told myself I needed so many. I sold all of them and went and bought myself a good quality purse that I use all the time. And I could go on.

I say all of this to say I know what discontentment can bring you. You are always saying "I will be happy when ..." but you won't be. You must learn to be content where you are right now. And when your neighbor gets that new lawn mower, tell them how great it is and smile while you use your push mower. Contentment will bring you joy. Contentment will erase jealousy. Contentment will put more money in your wallet. Remember, you get to write your own story. Make sure to include contentment in every chapter. Say goodbye to the Joneses.

> *"Content makes poor men rich; discontent makes rich men poor."*
>
> *Benjamin Franklin*

# K is for Kids and Money

*I* have a great question for you. Who is teaching your kids about money? Here's a hint: someone is, even if it isn't you. If it is not you, it is probably a friend, society, other family member, or a friend's parents. It may be you, even if you don't realize it. But I promise you, someone is teaching your kids about money. This is a parenting job, much like sex and morals, that has to be taught and should only be taught by you or someone you trust. Most parents don't feel comfortable talking about sex with their kids, but deep down they don't want their kids to learn about it from their friends. Personal finance is the same way. And just like sex and making life decisions, personal finance is a very important part of everyday life that can have major consequences if correct choices aren't made.

Now, the next great question is what are you teaching your kids about money? Many adults have trouble with their own personal finances and this can make them feel unqualified to teach their kids about money. However, as a parent it is your responsibility to teach your kids or make sure that are taught by a professional. If you are a parent who is struggling financially and is stressed out over money, you don't want to pass that on to your kids. If you are a parent who has it all together when it comes to money, you want to make sure you do pass that knowledge on to your kids. No matter what your own personal finances look like, we all want the same thing for our kids. We want them to be successful and never have to struggle when it comes to their personal finances. And there is only one thing we can do to help with this goal. We must teach our kids.

Teach is a verb that means "to cause to know how". We cannot simply tell our kids what to do and hope it sticks. We must teach them in great detail how to handle every aspect of their finances. You can't simply say "you have to save". You need to show them how to save (example: always take out 10%, before you do anything else, and invest it in your future) and show them why they need to do this. There are plenty of examples out there to show what can happen when you don't save and invest in your future. Use these examples as teaching moments. I learned something awesome at age 34 that I wish I had been shown at age 20. If you invest $100 a month from age 25 to age 65 in a growth stock mutual fund, you will have $ 1,188,000.00. This is valuable information. Most people, even kids, can save $100 a month. This is so simple, but this is information that is not taught. All we do is tell our kids "save, save, save". Kids (and adults for that matter) need a why.

Another important item to teach your children is that debt is not ok. Everywhere in society, they are being taught that debt is normal and just a part of life. We must stop teaching our kids that debt is necessary and start teaching them that they can live a better life without debt. In the workbook that accompanies this book is a great comparison you should share with your kids. It shows the difference in a "normal" young adult starting out and a "wise" young adult starting out (debt vs. no debt.) Did you know that 6 out of 10 kids between the ages of 18 and 39 are being helped financially by their parents? We are so busy trying to give our kids "stuff" that we are not focusing on helping them to become adults and financially responsible. This isn't fair to them, to the parents, or to the society that will have to help support them in the future. And it is not fair to our grandchildren, who will learn even less from their parents. We have to teach our kids. Kids have a blank slate when it comes to money. They only know what people tell them. How you handle money is not in your genes. It is in your teaching. Even if you feel like you can't teach them, make sure they receive good teaching through workshops, classes and books.

Now that I have shown you how important it is for you, the parent, to teach your kids about money, I want to help you with what to teach your kids about personal finance and when. Money talk is like sex talk. You need to always be talking about it and keeping the lines of communication open, but it always needs to be age appropriate. You wouldn't teach your 3 year old about investing, but you can teach him about saving.

Before I start with that information, I want to mention one more thing. As a parent, sometimes we have to humble ourselves and tell our kids we were wrong. If you haven't handled your personal finances well in the past, let your kids know that. Be honest with them about your actions. You don't have to share the details, but let them know you are gaining new knowledge about personal finances and you may have taught them some bad habits. Let them know you are sorry and you want to teach them a better way. You don't need to overdo it, but make sure they understand why changes are happening and that the changes are for the better. I have had to do this on more than one occasion. It was hard at first, but so worth it. I would rather be uncomfortable for a brief time than to have myself or my kid go through life with stress and pain.

### Age 3 to 6

In this age bracket, you are going to teach your kids some of the basics about money without a lot of detail. You can begin to pay them for a few chores or tasks that they are assigned to complete. Remember, at this age, it isn't about how good of a job that they do but that they do it. You are trying to show them how work equals money. If you don't work, you don't get paid. Money is not just handed to them.

At this age and beyond, it is important to show them how to give, save, and spend. Also teach them why each is important. They need to give because they need to know that everything isn't about them. They should also help people who are in need and have less than them. They need to save for the future and in case they have an emergency. And then they need to know that what is left over is what they can spend. But they also need to learn the money is finite. There is no money tree. What they have is what they have and they need to make choices with it. A quick word of advice – this will be hard at times. They will have to learn the hard way and it is important to not bail them out. No parent wants to watch their kid make a mistake or cry when they do. But it is very important to the teaching process that you don't give in and you don't help, in most cases. No one likes to hear the word no – adults or kids. But we have to learn to be okay with that word. It is better for them to learn it at this age because it will just get harder the older they get.

### Age 7 to 12

This is a hard age in most areas. This is the time when many kids start to lose some of their innocence and begin to have very strong opinions about things. This is also the ages where they begin to gain confidence in their knowledge, many times too much confidence. If you are starting the money talk at this age, you need to realize that you will probably have a challenging start because some money habits have already been formed just by their observation of you and the people in their lives. If you have been teaching money since an early age, there will still be challenges, but it won't be as difficult for them to understand because hopefully they will have started to develop good money habits already.

The main thing you need to know is that everyone is different. We all learn different and process what we know differently. The main goal for you is to get good common sense knowledge into your kids so that they can make good choices in the future. Therefore, don't be upset if they don't do something exactly like you would do it or make the exact decision you would. There is more than one way to skin a cat, as my grandma would always say.

As your kids begin the tween years, it is very important to begin including them in some of the family money decisions. Let me give an example to clarify. If you are planning for a vacation, they can help you to shop for the best hotels and help you with the budget for the trip. However, they don't have the final say in where you go and what your budget will be. It is okay to tell them how much the budget is for certain items and explain that you are paying cash and you will need to stick to the budget that you come up with. They can also contribute with an itinerary for the trip that includes dollar amounts beside each item. This will help them to see that money is finite and needs to be respected, but if you save you can do the things that you want to do. It will also be a great lesson in choices, deciding what is most important to them and to the family. You need to choose what decisions are okay for them to have a say in because not all money decisions are appropriate to discuss at this age. For example, kids should not have a say in buying a home, car, or any luxury item. They do not have enough knowledge at this age to make these decisions and their decisions would be based strictly on their wants, not what is wise and best.

As at any age, you need to keep talking about money. Not too much and not too little, but just right for your kid. Begin to talk to them a lot about the why at this age. Why we work, why we save, why we give, and why they want the things that they want. Also, begin to help them think outside the box about money decisions. And lastly, without judging or putting other people down, help them to learn from other people's mistakes. Mostly explain why that wouldn't have been a choice you would have made.

## *Age 13 to 18*

Now we are at the fun age. If you are there, as I am, you know what I mean. If you are not, hold on. This is the time where your kid believes they know everything. They honestly believe that their 13 or so years on this earth have gained them all of the knowledge they need to get through life. And this is not a new concept. I believed the exact same thing when I was 13. You couldn't tell me anything. I knew it all. Of course, now I know I wasn't anywhere close to knowing anything. There are times now, with my daughter, that I laugh at her reaction and comment to things but I also know the importance of not blowing them off. You see, she actually believes what she is saying. Her brain is not fully developed and won't be until about the age of 23, but her world is about making adult decisions. I am very lucky to have a very open relationship with my daughter. Unfortunately, I can't make her decisions for her, but I can use mistakes from my life and examples to guide her and let her know the consequences, both good and bad, of all of the choices available.

There is one huge element missing from our children today. They do not understand how what they do today is connected to their tomorrow. Our kids are living day by day and having no thought about the future. An example of this is with sex (even though that isn't what this book is about). They don't understand the emotions attached and the true consequences of their actions. They have no idea what this will mean when they are in their 20's and want to get married. They are living for the moment and have no idea of the regret that will come in the future. They also truly believe that the bad couldn't possibly happen to them. Again, they have all of the answers.

Just like money and sex and other topics, we have to be continuously talking to our kids and helping them with this. These are the formidable years. Your mistakes will be worth everything you went through if you can keep your kids from making the same ones. This will take humility and honesty on your part and maybe some embarrassment but it is all worth it to keep your kids on the right path.

This is the age where they need to begin to make their own money. Please don't let your kid graduate high school having never earned a dime. It is healthy for them to take on a part time job or start their own little business and begin to associate work with money. At age 13 to 15, they can baby sit, cut lawns, and walk dogs to earn some money. At age 15 and up, they can do those things or take on a little part time job to earn some money. It is at this time that the personal finance lessons need to really kick up. There is a lot to learn before they go out on their own and it is important that they gain that knowledge as early and as often as they can.

I want to list some of the things that are important for them to gain knowledge on at this age. There are resources available to help you if you need it. Some schools teach personal finance, unfortunately teaching that debt is okay. We offer workshops and one-on-one tutoring in person, via phone, or Skpe. There are also other great authors and teachers out there if you need help, but make sure your teen gets this information. It could really make or break them. They need to learn:

- ❖ How taxes work – whether self-employed or working for a company
- ❖ How to budget – even at this age, they have money coming in and money they want to spend.
- ❖ How to give and save in addition to spending.

❖ How banking works – from opening the right account to how a debit card works to balancing a checkbook (old school).

❖ How to buy a used car with cash and what other expenses are included with it (insurance, gas, yearly fees, etc.)

❖ How debt works and why it is not wise. If you are going to teach them debt is okay, be honest about the fees and interest you are paying to have something before you can afford it. Make sure they understand that they are reaching into their uncertain future to have something today.

❖ How to find their passion for their future. It is important that they live to work, not work to live. We want our children to do what they love doing and be able to make an income at it. Help and guide them with this.

This is just the beginning to the knowledge that teens need to gain during this time of their lives. But it is crucial. I know how much I wish I had this knowledge when I was growing up. The unfortunate thing is I don't think I would have realized it back then. A big challenge you will face is getting your teen interested in the subject of how to handle money. They love money, but not the physics of it. Take baby steps if necessary, but make sure your teen gains this knowledge. Unfortunately, some of it will be gained through pain. Make sure you are there for them even then, not to bail them out or to say I told you so, but to bestow on them a teachable moment.

## College or Life

At this point in their lives they are going to be deciding about their futures. Let me start out this next section by saying that higher education is a privilege and not a right. Only 57% of students who go to college finish, leaving 43% to never finish. College isn't for everyone and that is okay. Young adults (and some adults) are automatically going to college using student loans without having a clue what they want to do with their lives. The most important career path is the path that takes you to your passion. Work is a part of life and will be there for most of your days. No one wants to be miserable their whole life, yet so many people are currently. Many people go to work everyday just so they can pay off their debt and pay for "stuff". Is your "stuff" really worth your misery?

Everyone has something that they enjoy and a gift that they can use to make themselves and others happy. To many people, this is considered a hobby, not a career. But you could make a career out of a hobby. Every passion can be turned into an income. The first, most important step, to helping your young adult decide their life path is to help them identify their passion and then how to monetize that passion.

Now, if that passion requires higher education, teaching for example, then the next step is to be wise in how we obtain that higher education. Student loans are not "good" debt. They are debt that has to be paid back, with interest, at the worst time in a person life, just when they are starting out. The last thing you need when you are starting a new career and single life is debt. Nothing is more crippling than that. And contrary to popular belief, you can obtain your higher education without any student loans. A great book to read on this subject is by Zac Bissonnette entitled "Debt Free U". Below are also a few things that have worked for me and other people along the way.

- ❖ If a parent can contribute and has saved to pay cash, they can do so. A parent should not go into debt or ever cosign (we will cover in a minute) a loan for college.

❖ Choose a local, in state college or public college to attend. The education you will receive will be equivalent to a more expensive college somewhere else. The purpose of college is simply to obtain the knowledge necessary for the career you have chosen. Knowledge is knowledge and it won't be any better at a more expensive school. Most companies do not choose the candidates based on which school they went to, they choose them based on their knowledge and understanding of their field.

❖ You can go to a community college for the first two years and then transfer to a local college for the last two years. In the first two years of your college education, you are only learning the basic courses needed for your degree. It isn't until year three that you begin to really focus on your core courses. So save yourself the money and get what you need in the best way. Make sure the college you want to attend in year three will accept all of the courses from the community college.

❖ You can work your way through college. It is possible to work 40 hours a week and go to school full time. Many people do it. It doesn't leave time for partying but you are not in school to party. You are in school to learn. My step daughter used to work two jobs in the summer and save every penny to pay for the next year. Currently, it is $18,000 to attend Clemson University per year in state tuition. This includes meals and books but not room and board. That is $1,500 per month. When you break it down like that, it becomes doable between parents contribution (if any) and what the student can earn.

❖ Apply for every grant and scholarship available. There are thousands of local and national grants and scholarships that you can apply for each year. Spend time applying for as many as you can. If you received ten $300 scholarships, that is $3,000 of free money. If you apply for hundreds even thousands, you increase the number you are likely to get. Apply for them even if they are small amounts. They add up and every little bit helps.

❖ Look for out of the box schools to attend. College of the Ozarks in Missouri doesn't charge tuition to its full time students thanks to donations and the student work program. All students must work 15 hours per week somewhere on campus and two 40 hour weeks a year. The work they do provides items for the school to sell which pays for the tuition. This school focuses on hard work and building character. The college is also debt free so all of the money they make can go toward the student's education.

We have become and are raising our kids to become an entitlement society. We believe that we are entitled to something just because we exist. And this is just not true. You can have anything you want if you work hard, use out of the box thinking, always use wisdom, and know that today is connected to tomorrow.

### Cosigning

I get asked more questions about cosigning than any other thing. And mostly is relates to ones kids. So I think now is the appropriate time to discuss this very important subject. We all want to help our kids and many parents think an easy way is to cosign for them. We tell ourselves we are helping them, but you couldn't be further from the truth.

It is never okay to cosign for anyone and here is why. First, why does someone need a cosigner in the first place? It is because the bank or lending institution believes that the person is not going to pay them back. And the odds are they are right. When they miss a payment or are late with a payment, it not only affects them, it affects your credit as well. At this point, your relationship becomes very uncomfortable. And many times can't be healed. It has the same effect relationally as borrowing money from family and that is a big no no. Proverbs, which is a book of wise sayings, states that "The borrower is a slave to the lender." And because your name and credit are on the line, your child is a slave to you and the bank. An article just came out this week about how many social security recipients are having their social security checks garnished up to 15% due to defaulted student loans. These are mostly people who cosigned for their kids or grandkids and they are not making the payments. Therefore, the parent or grandparent is responsible and they don't have the money either. Many social security recipients are living paycheck to paycheck and this is just making it worse. But we never think this far when we are trying to help by cosigning.

There is a solution here if you want to help them. First, make sure you are helping them and not enabling them.

Many times we think we are solving a problem when we are just putting a band aid on it.  But if you believe that your money can help them, then give it too them.  And only give what you can afford to give.   And then let it go.  Never hold it over them again or remind them of it.  If you were wrong, and it didn't help them, don't keep bringing it up.  Just learn from that mistake and never repeat it.

Love your kids enough to say no.  Love your kids enough to teach them about something as important as money.  Love your kids enough to help them find their passion, not just a job.  Love your kids enough to talk them through their mistakes, not remind them of them.  Love your kids.

> "Do not exasperate your children; instead bring them up in the training and instruction of the Lord."
> Ephesians 6:4

# L is for Life and Legacy

*T*wo questions:  What kind of life are you living now and what legacy are you hoping to leave when you depart from us?  If you believe, as we discussed in the previous chapter, that life is a continuum, every decision you make today will affect your tomorrow.  What would occur if you left us today (Lord willing you won't)?  Would your family be able to grieve and not worry about their future or would they be left to grieve and to stress out financially?

My best advice to widows and widowers is to take a year to grieve and not make any major decisions.  But many times, they are forced to make these decisions based on the legacy left to them.  This chapter will focus on life now and decisions that should be made to insure a great legacy in the future.  Here's a hint:  A great legacy is not about the amount of money you leave your family.  You can leave them a great legacy even without leaving them millions.

## *Snapshot*

Take a moment now to take a snapshot of your life. Luckily for us, life is a movie not a snapshot, but snapshots can help us to see where we are presently. Let's ask ourselves a few questions about our snapshot to see if we are where we need to be.

❖ How much retirement savings do you have? Retirement can be inherited in the event that you should leave us early. This makes it not only vital for your future, but the future of your family. You should be putting away around 15% to 18% per year into growth stock mutual funds and retirement accounts such as 401K's, especially if your employer does a match. This wise financial decision is helpful to both your life now and your legacy.

❖ How much life insurance do you have? Life insurance is one of the most important insurances to carry on yourself. I have seen this make a life impact, both having it and not having it. You want to make sure you have the right amount and right type so that you get the most for your money. We covered, in detail, the types and amounts of life insurance you should have on yourself and your spouse in a previous chapter. But to summarize, you should have a term life insurance policy on you for the amount of ten times your annual income. If you do not produce an income, you need about $400,000 of coverage on you. Life is never guaranteed for any of us and your health could change overnight. It is wise to get this insurance today in order to leave a lasting legacy.

❖ Do you have a will and power of attorney? Everyone needs these two items, whether you have assets or not and whether you are married or not. You need someone you trust to have the power to act on your behalf in any situation that you are not able to. Just because you are legally married does not mean that your spouse has a complete say over items regarding you. Once you are 18 years of age, it is imperative to have these two legal items drawn up. You can do a Power of Attorney or simple will from between $30 and $50. If you have a lot of assets, you may need to set up a trust, especially if you have children, and this would need to be done by a trust attorney. Either way, make sure that there is no doubt of your wishes on everything once you have left us. Telling someone verbally is great, but not enough. According to Smart Money Magazine, 70% of adults do not have a will. It is wise to get a will and power of attorney not only for your life now, but for a lasting legacy.

### *Legacy Book*

In a drawer in my desk, is a binder full of everything my husband or I will need in the event of death. This is called our "Legacy Book". In our family, as in many families, I am the bookkeeper. We always make financial decisions together, but I execute them by writing the checks or filing the paperwork. It is hard enough to keep all of the accounts, passwords and wishes in check while we are alive, but when we are grieving it is almost impossible. This is where the "Legacy Book" is vital. This can take on any form you want and be located anywhere you want it to be, but it is crucial to have. This way, your spouse and children know exactly how to keep the finances going and what they need to know and deal with. Below are just some of the important things to have in your "Legacy Book":

- ❖ All life insurance policies – numbers, name of company and amounts.
- ❖ All bank account information – bank and account numbers and any passwords needed. This also includes safety deposit box information and key location.
- ❖ All retirement account information – companies, account numbers and balances.
- ❖ A copy of your will – the original should be in your safety deposit box or in a lockbox.
- ❖ A copy of your power of attorney – same as above, the original should be kept in a safety deposit box or in a lockbox.
- ❖ All mortgage information – company, account number, and balance. The deed should be in your safety deposit box or lockbox.
- ❖ A list of all of your debts – company, account numbers, and balances.
- ❖ If you are over 65, social security information. The surviving spouse is allowed to collect the higher of the two amounts. Therefore you need the information on both of you in order to process that request.

- ❖ The name of your lawyer, accountant, financial advisor and the executor of your estate – this will help the beneficiaries to know who to contact about your estate and wishes.

- ❖ A list of all usernames and passwords for any computers, email and websites you may use. For example, I use our bank's website for online banking. I would need to list the website and the username and password for my spouse.

- ❖ A list of your funeral wishes and the deed to your burial plot, if you have purchased it already. You should discuss these wishes with your spouse and family, but it needs to be written down as well.

- ❖ Deeds to any other property (second home, boat, cars, etc.) you own – originals should be kept in a safety deposit box or lock box and a copy made for the file.

This is just a beginners list to get you started. As with anything else, you need to tailor it to your personal situation. The "Legacy Book" should contain within it any and everything that your spouse or family could possibly need in the event of your death. It is better to have too much information than not enough.

This chapter is the shortest so far, but is still very important. Your legacy is more than the amount of money your leave your children. Your legacy is how you live your life now and what you do to take care of them in the future. Your life and legacy should motivate you to get out of debt in order to give to future generations. The legacy and example you will leave future generations about how you respect your money is the best legacy you could ever leave. Live your best life and that will be your greatest legacy.

> "Your story is the greatest legacy that you will leave to your friends. It's the longest-lasting legacy you will leave to your heirs."
>
> Steve Saint

# M is for Marriage and Money

*I* could write an entire book (and probably will someday) on the subject of marriage and money. It is the biggest issue that I counsel on and the largest cause of divorce in this country. 52% of Americans are divorced and about 80% of those divorces occurred due to financial issues. And from my observation, the biggest financial issue is not actual currency (or lack of it), but is communication and compromise when it comes to household finances.

One of the best books I have ever read on the subject of marriage is "Love and Respect" by Dr. Emerson Eggerichs. In it he explains how a man's greatest desire is for respect and a woman's greatest desire is for love. I have found this to be true in most of my counseling sessions. Men want to be respected as the head of the house and women want to feel loved by having their opinion matter. There have been several great books written to explain why men and women are so different. I think it is great that we are different. If all we did was marry a replica of ourselves, we would get very bored very quickly.  This is where the art of compromise and communication can make all the difference in your marriage.

You cannot always be right and you can't always get your way and remain happily married.  It is not fair to you or your spouse.  If you were always right and got your way all the time, you would become very selfish and self absorbed.  If your spouse always had to be right and always had to get their way, you would become bitter.  So, therefore, it is imperative to find the middle ground.

As a counselor and coach, I push pre-marriage counseling on every engaged couple I meet or come in contact with.  I truly believe there would be far less divorces if this counseling occurred.  The reason it is so important to me is because there are four areas of your lives that must be in agreement in order to sustain the challenges of marriage:  kids, religion, finances, and family (in-laws).  You don't have to agree 100%, but you need to take the time to find out, in depth, what your fiancés beliefs are in these major areas of life.  Here's an example I come across a lot.  Let's say you do not believe in debt.  Either you had debt and paid it off or you have never had any and don't intend to start now.  Now, let's say your fiancé has debt. That alone is not a reason to break off the engagement. But now let's say he has debt, uses credit cards, buys a new car using debt every 4 years and has no intention of stopping just because you don't like debt. At this point, these conflicting attitudes become a major problem. Not that either of you is right or wrong, but having such different views on money is going to cause continuous money fights and strife throughout your entire marriage. You know that I am opposed to debt and by now you know why, but if both of you agree to have debt your entire life, I will not tell you to not get married. The reason is that even though I don't agree with you, you are on the same page and that is what is important here.

If you are already married, don't think you are off the hook. You may not have gotten the pre-marriage counseling that you should have, but it is never to late to start a conversation. I challenge you, if you are married and have never had this conversation, that you have it today. It is never too late to share your beliefs, ideas and dreams and to get on the same page regarding your personal finances.

Once you have had this conversation, whether before or after the ceremony, you are basically left with two choices, if you find out that you are on two completely different pages. You can discuss your differences, talk out why you believe what you do and come to a compromise that is mutually beneficial to you both. This may require counseling or mediation to help you talk it through without causing defenses to go up. Remember, love and respect. And, of course the second choice is to give up. I don't recommend this. You married each other for a reason and hopefully the big reason was love. So you need to always keep that at the front of your mind as you are trying to get on the same page regarding your finances or any of the other areas we discussed.

Proverbs 17:1 says *"Better a dry crust with peace and quiet than a house full of feasting, with strife."* No one sets out to be miserable their whole life. Yet there are many people in that exact place right now. In many cases, they have chosen strife over peace. As I said before, but it is worth repeating, you do not always have to be right. And even if you are right, you don't always have to point it out. Dale Carnegie, in his great book "How to Win Friends and Influence People", shared a personal story of his that changed the way he dealt with people forever. Here is the idea of the story.

> *Dale was at a dinner party with a dear friend given by an acquaintance of his. During the course of the meal, Dale was seated between his friend and the host of the party. The host was telling a story and used a quote that he said was from the Bible. Dale knew that it wasn't and proceeded to correct him. They argued back and forth and finally decided to let the other friend settle it for them, as he was a professor of Shakespeare and Dale knew that it came from one of Shakespeare's plays. When they posed the question to the friend, the friend politely nudged Dale under the table and told the host that he was correct and it was from the Bible. On their way home, Dale asked his friend why he had done that. His friend said that the host was convinced that he was right and nothing anyone said was going to change his mind. In addition, it was his party and it was rude to embarrass him in such a manner.*

What Dale learned that night changed him. He realized that he didn't need to always be right, even if sometimes he was.  From then on, he picked when it was necessary to correct people, but found that most of the time, he just left it alone.

You see, you will never win an argument with your spouse, even if you are right.  In the book of Jonah, Jonah wanted so bad to be right that he was willing to die if God wouldn't recognize him as being right.  Are you willing to lose a happy marriage in order to always be right?  You need to learn to appreciate your differences and work with them, not use them against each other.

### *Marriage Money*

As I said before, it is not usually the money that destroys marriages.  It is a greedy, selfish heart.  Unfortunately, this trait can show up in many levels in us and is not visible in a mirror.  No one would ever speak up and say "Why yes, of course I am selfish and have a greedy heart."  As we said in a previous chapter, greed is the assumption that everything is for your consumption.  And, of course, we all know what selfish looks like.  We see it in other people every day.  I am not going to ask you to decide if you are greedy or selfish.  That is between you and the good Lord.  But if you are, it will come out in many ways and forms.

Let me ask you a question.  How are your family finances handled?  I am not talking about the money itself, whether you live within your means or not, but how are the day to day decisions and bookkeeping handled.  When the preacher said "You are now one", he didn't just mean your name.  This includes everything.  And he didn't mean that one of you controls everything and the other just sits back and does nothing.

"You are now one" includes your finances and your stuff as much as anything else.  This means that the accounts you have will have both of your names on them, the things you buy will be in both of your names, and that all financial decisions will be discussed and compromised on together.  Marriages who have one checking account in each individuals names and one joint account will not work.  Marriages who have one controlling spouse and one subservient spouse will not work.  Marriages where one spouse cares for their "toy" over their willingness to share their "toy" will not work.  True and happy marriages are built on trust, sharing and putting the other person before yourself. Selfishness and greed have no place in a marriage and will never bring happiness to that marriage.

So, how do you handle your marriage money in a way that both parties are happy and is best for both? Here are a few musts to start:

- ❖ Every bank account has both names listed on them and both spouses have access to them. There cannot be any hidden money anywhere. Everything you had is now your spouse's and vice versa.

- ❖ Everything includes your debts as well as your assets. When you marry your spouse, you marry them knowing what their financial situation is and accepting it. Therefore, their debt is now yours and vice versa. You do not need to add your name to the other person's accounts unless you are continuing to use them. If you are paying them off in order to get out of debt, you don't need to add your name. You need to just mentally know that they are your debts now, also, and never say "If it wasn't for your student loan, we wouldn't be broke."

❖ Everything you own belongs to the other person as well now. You no longer can say "my car" or "my stamp collection" or "my house". Everything becomes "our". The only thing you definitely add your spouse's name to is the deed of your house. Everything else is up to you and your spouse.

❖ Both of you have an equal voice in all financial decisions. Not one person always gets their way. And you need to learn the great art of compromise because it is the best tool you need in any happy marriage.

These are just a few of the most important items to start. The word "our" will become a key word in your marriage and in talking with other people and your kids. This lets people know you are a team and that the decisions and choices you are making are with mutual respect. There is not a better example of marriage that you can show to your kids, family and the world as that.

### *Financial Infidelity*

Most people, if asked, would tell you they would never even think of committing infidelity. However, there is a growing trend of financial infidelity in marriages. You may not have ever heard of such a thing but it strongly exists. Infidelity is marital disloyalty and financial infidelity is being disloyal when it comes to money. More financial transactions are hidden today than ever before.

This action can stem from several things. One is a sense that a spouse's voice is not being heard. When a person feels that their opinion and wants about the finances is never considered, they will soon act out by doing what they want behind their spouse's back. They will begin to buy things and hide the receipts and shopping bags and in turn, lie about where they have been and what they have been doing. Another thing that makes a person hide transactions from their spouse is because of a feeling of financial abuse. I, of course, am not talking about something physical or even verbal, but I am talking about one spouse controlling the other. This is done many times through one spouse being in charge of all of the finances and then giving the other spouse an "allowance" for what they may need. When a person feels like they are being controlled, they will lie and hide in order to get what they need.

The biggest reason I have seen recently for financial infidelity is one spouse putting the entire financial burden on the other spouse. A common example of this is a wife, who is a stay at home mom, and the husband is the sole bread winner. The husband figures it is her job to take care of everything including the finances. The finances become overwhelming, especially if there is no budgeting or organization, and she begins to get behind. She then begins to make it worse by opening credit cards and taking out loans to catch up. Usually it will finally get so bad that she breaks down and tells the husband about the loans and credit cards. And of course, he is furious. Now, he should feel betrayed that she went behind his back and did what she did. But he is not off of the hook. Remember, he dumped it all on her and basically said "have at it."

All of these reasons could be avoided by working together on the finances. It is neither fair nor loving to give (or take) sole responsibility to one spouse. Marriage is always a team effort. This may sound harsh, but if you don't want to be part of a team, stay single. When you make the decision to marry the person you love most in this world, you need to spend everyday respecting them as well.

Just like you would want to take all of the necessary steps to avoid marital infidelity (an affair), you will also want to take steps to avoid financial infidelity.

❖ Step 1 – Always let both parties voice be heard. There should never be one spouse always getting their way and the other person always giving in. If the wife wants a dress, try to come up with a plan together to get her that dress. If the dress is too much, try to compromise and set a budget for a new dress. If the husband wants to get a new television, same rules apply. Sometimes one person may get their way first, but the next time you can switch off. That happens to me and my husband a lot. First, we prioritize but if what we are wanting are just "wants", then we take turns. This way nobody feels unheard and left out.

❖ Step 2 – Set up a guardrail that you will never do anything financial that your spouse doesn't know about. My husband and I each get a little "mad money" every week. That is ours to do as we wish, no discussion necessary. But everything above that is, at the very least, discussed and an agreement is made or we don't do it.

❖ Step 3 – Put yourself in the other person's shoes. If your spouse did to you what you are thinking about doing to them, would you like it? Of course not. There is no pair of shoes, clothes, or electronic gadget that is worth the trust of your spouse.

Here's a great question for you. Do you know your spouse's story? Everybody does what they do for a reason. Before you get mad at your spouse for their way of thinking, try to find out why they think that way. I will reiterate. Pre-marriage counseling is a must for helping you get your spouse's story. If you are already married, take the time now to not only find out your spouse's story but to share your story. Understanding and sharing why we do something the way we do it, will help us to work with the other person to reach common goals.

None of us gets married with the intention of having unhappy marriages or getting divorced. Yet over 52% of couples are divorced and I would bet about 70% are unhappy. Most of this unhappiness shows up in the financial realm because it can be the most stressful.

From my own personal experience, I would like to give some unsolicited advice. Please don't get married unless you are absolutely sure you are in love and can spend the rest of your life with someone. You need to love them in spite of their faults and don't hold those faults against them. And also make sure you get the proper counseling before taking such a big step.

Wisdom in buying a house is knowing everything from what you can afford to where you get the most house for your money. Wisdom in getting married is knowing everything from his/her faults to what political party they are. Know everything you can possibly know about someone before you marry them and always marry for the right reason – love. I can look back now and know everything that went wrong in my first marriage and it wasn't just the other person. I wasn't wise in my decision and I realized too late that there were just some things I couldn't live with. That didn't make him a bad person. It just meant we weren't meant for each other. I learned from that and have gotten it right this time from start to finish. Yes, we have disagreements. Yes, we have heated discussions. But at the end of the day, we always work it out. I have learned I don't always have to be right, even if I am. I don't always have to get my way. And at the end of the day, my love for my husband is more important than any "thing" that I could ever obtain. If you realize you married the wrong person, it may not be too late for you. Get some counseling and try to work it out together. Odds are you love each other on some level or you never would have married in the first place. Remember, in every aspect of your life, including your finances, men desire respect and women desire love.

> *"Each one of you also must love his wife as he loves himself, and the wife must respect her husband."*
> *Ephesians 5:33*

# N is for Need vs. Want

*I* have realized that we, for the most part, find it hard to recognize a need from a want. A need is anything that is required for you to exist. A want is everything else. An even larger problem I have realized is that we are prioritizing our financial lives to cover our wants first and then our needs. It is because of this error in priorities that many people are where they are today. Let's take a moment to look at a surface difference in needs and wants.

- ❖ You need shelter. You want a house with all of the bells and whistles.
- ❖ You need food. You want pizza, steaks, to eat out, soda, etc.
- ❖ You need clothes. You want new, name brand clothes every season.
- ❖ You need transportation. This could be anything from a bicycle to a car, but you don't need a brand new car.
- ❖ You need utilities. You want cable and internet.

I hope you can begin to see where I am going with this. I am just as bad about this as anyone. I have to, many times, think about what is a real need and what is a want. I catch myself all of the time saying to a store clerk, "I need a soda, please." I no more need a soda than I need a hole in my head. But I think I do because I am thirsty and I have always been able to afford the luxury of a soda when I wanted one. This is something we say all of the time. "We need a vacation." "I need a new purse." You do not require a vacation to live and you don't need a new purse to survive. We really need to begin to recognize what is a want and what is a need. This doesn't mean you can't have your wants. If you can afford them, you can have all of the wants you desire. But it is imperative as we move through life to recognize the difference so that we can prioritize our lives as well as teach our children the difference. By the way, "afford" doesn't mean using a credit card or going into debt for things. Afford means that all of your needs and obligations are met and you have cash left over. At that time, you may decide to buy a want and that is okay. But if you are in debt, you have already reached into your future to buy your wants. You need to pay off those "wants" before you purchase anymore.

## *Extra Money*

What would you say if I told you that you have extra money? Would you think I am crazy? Would you say no way? Here are a few questions you can answer to see if you have extra money or not:

- ❖ Do you have extra change in your car right now?
- ❖ Did you eat out this week, either fast food or in a sit down restaurant?
- ❖ Did you go to the movies, rent a movie or do any other recreational activity this week?
- ❖ Do you own more than one car or a recreational vehicle such as a boat?
- ❖ Did you buy a purse, pair of shoes, video game or any other fun item recently?

Basically, if you are able to do anything above and beyond your needs (your real needs), you have extra money. Most people don't realize this concept, however, because all of their extra money is spent before they even make it (i.e. debt). People are living paycheck to paycheck, but not because they don't make enough money or that their necessities cost more than they make. People are living paycheck to paycheck because they have made so many promises on future money that at the end of it all, there is no money left each month. Most of the people working today are working to pay off their wants.

If you made a list of your actual needs, you would find that you make plenty of money to cover them. If you then made a list of all of your monthly bills, you would see that your "extra money", the money above what it takes to meet those needs, is used on wants. You see, you have the money to save for retirement. You have the money to invest in a college fund for your child. You have the money to put into savings to have a 6-8 month emergency fund. You also have the money to pay for your true wants in cash. But when you mortgage your future earnings in order to get all of your wants now, you will never see your extra money.

Your basic needs are:

❖ Shelter based on what you can afford. If all you can afford right now is a one bedroom apartment, then that is all you need. Shelter is a roof over your head. I have lived in everything from a room in someone's basement to an apartment to owning a home. Where I lived was based on what I could afford, wisely, to do.

❖ Food is necessary, but eating out isn't. When I was just starting out, I ate Ramen noodles, bologna, and macaroni and cheese. Hopefully you can do better than this, but again food is based on what you can afford.

❖ Clothing is a must, but it doesn't have to be fancy. If you have enough outfits for a week, along with underwear and one to two pairs of shoes, that is all you need. I, still today, shop in local thrift stores for some of our clothes.

❖ Utilities are a necessity, but only electric and water. Telephone, cell phones, cable and internet are not necessary to live.

❖ Transportation of some kind is necessary in most cases. However, a good estate sale car will get you to work and back which is all that is necessary.

If you look at your finances through this lens, which will be new to most of you, you will see that the majority of your money is going towards wants. And hopefully when you can see the potential extra money that could be available to you, you will put your wants on hold, pay off the wants you have already bought, and reevaluate your finances based on needs first.

### *I Want It All*

What I really want you to get out of this chapter is the difference in a need and a want. But I also want you to understand that it is okay to have wants and to have them fulfilled, but it needs to be done in a way that is wise and a blessing. I want you to understand that you do not need cable or the internet. You do not need a cell phone. You do not need a new car. You do not need clothes from the mall. It is imperative to understand this difference or you will never get ahead and build wealth.

Psalms 37:4 tells us very clearly that God wants to give us the desires of our heart. God wants you to have what you want, but your stuff can't come first. So many people today put all of their wants before their needs because their lives are all about their "stuff". Do you go to work everyday because you love what you do or do you go to work everyday to pay for your "stuff"? I worked for 15 years of my life for "stuff". I have worked jobs I hated or held jobs with immoral companies all because of my "stuff". I didn't find true freedom until I got my "stuff" under control. I now have the privilege to do what I love to do everyday of my life. I get to help people and teach. That brings me more joy than any purse ever could.

Hebrews 13:5 says *"Keep your lives free from the love of money and be content with what you have, because God has said, 'Never will I leave you; never will I forsake you.'"* God will always meet your real needs. This is a promise for everyone, whether you believe in God or not. Does a bird worry about where his next meal will come from or where he will sleep? Have you ever seen a stressed out bird? The answer is no because God promises to provide for the bird just as he will provide for you (Matthew 6:26). You can't not have an "I want it and I want it now" attitude. That is for two year olds. In order for your wants to be a blessing, you have to obtain them after your needs and with wisdom and patience.

Now you may be saying "Debbi, I don't believe in that God stuff." But let me ask you this. Have you ever prayed for something to do with money? Have you ever prayed that a deal would go through such as the sell of a house or the loan on a car? On some level, I think we all believe there is something out there bigger than us and when we want something, we call out to that bigger being. If you are going to ask for something, however, the best thing you can ask for is wisdom, not stuff. God doesn't want your stuff. He wants to make sure your stuff doesn't get you.

### *Satisfaction*

Are you currently satisfied? If I looked at your bank statements and all of your debt statements, would I believe you are satisfied? If you are never satisfied, you will never obtain wealth. Being satisfied means being happy and content with what you have already and not constantly figuring out how to get more. As I have said before, we have become an upgrade society in contrast to the replacement society we used to be. A couple of decades ago, people bought things, even things that they wanted not just needed, and they kept them until they completely broke and couldn't be fixed anymore. Then they replaced them. Now a days, we replace something just because we want the latest and greatest, the newest fad. A lot of this stems from discontentment which is fueled by awareness. If you weren't aware that there was something cooler and more hip out there, you would be satisfied with what you have. But because you are always seeing the latest and greatest on television, in magazines, and through your family and friends, you are very aware and this leads to discontentment and dissatisfaction.

One of the biggest keys to wealth is a state of contentment and satisfaction. If you can't be happy with where you are and what you have, you will always be spending everything you make on trying to reach satisfaction. And just when you think you have reached it, something new will come along. Don't hide behind such thoughts as "I need a new car" or "I have to have a new pair of shoes". My minivan has 413,000 miles on it. When something breaks, I get it repaired and move on. I do not need a new car. Only when the van can't be fixed anymore will I need another car. And at that time, I will buy, new or used, only what I can afford in cash.

The Israelites were in the desert for 40 years. During this learning journey that they were on, they never once needed new shoes. Their shoes and clothes lasted them for 40 years. I am not saying you have to keep a pair of shoes or your clothes for 40 years. The point of this entire chapter is very simple but vitally important. You have to be truthful about the difference in a need and a want. You must make sure all of your needs are taken care of and then proceed to your wants, little by little. If you want to have true satisfaction and wealth, when something wears out, ask yourself (and be truthful) can this be repaired? If it can, do so. And when it can't, use wisdom to obtain what you want within your financial means. Sometimes you may want something new before what you have wears out. It is okay to move forward with that purchase as long as it is done wisely and with extra money, not money for needs.

Girl Scouts can now earn badges for an array of money skills. They added these badges because "There was a lot of interest on the part of the girls in how to have the money for the things they need to do in life." says Eileen Doyle, vice-president of programs. For 9-year old Laurel Petrides the take-away is something we all need to think about next time we go to buy something. "If you spend on something you want first, then you might not have enough for what you need." I couldn't have said it better myself.

> "This is what I have observed to be good: that it is appropriate for a person to eat, to drink and to find satisfaction in their toilsome labor under the sun during the few days of life God has given them—for this is their lot. Moreover, when God gives someone wealth and possessions, and the ability to enjoy them, to accept their lot and be happy in their toil—this is a gift of God."
>
> *Ecclesiastes 5:18-19*

# O is for Out of Balance

*7* hroughout this book, we have talked about many things that cause us to have financial stress and difficulties. Being out of balance, financially, is a big one. Being out of balance financially not only affects your finances, but affects many other aspects of your life such as your marriage or your job. Being out of balance is the major reason for the economic situation of this country and its citizens. Balance is a necessity of life and of personal finance.

First, let's look at what being in balance, in anything, looks like. There are always extremes, either one direction or another. In between the extremes is the middle and in the middle you will find balance. Many people never find their balance. Our objective is to not only find our balance but to always be maintaining that balance. Like with many other areas of your personal finances, keeping balance is an ongoing lifestyle, not a one time deal. Balance, in personal finance, has four components: spending, saving, giving, and working. If you have too much of one of these components and not enough of the others, you will be out of balance. For example, if your only goal is to work and make as much money as you can, your personal life and family will suffer. It is a great goal to make as much money as possible in your field of work, but it has to be done with balance. The same effect will be true if you save as much as you can, give as much as you can or spend as much as you can. Any one of these components done in extreme by itself will cause great unbalance. You have to find a nice balance between all four components.

There are three main steps to take in order to maintain balance in anything, including the four components discussed above. To explain the steps for maintaining balance, we must first envision a tight rope walker. The tightrope walker must maintain his balance from one side to the other and if he doesn't, the consequence is big. The following steps will help him maintain his balance to the other side and will help you maintain balance between spending, saving, giving, and working.

❖ **Step 1** – The tightrope walker must have a reference point. If he doesn't have a goal and keep his eye on the goal, he will fall. For the tightrope walker, this reference point is the other side. As he walks across the rope, he never takes his eye off of the other side.  If he does, he will begin to lose his balance and he could fall.

In your finances, your reference point is your spending plan or budget.  Your budget should always represent your income (working) and your expenses (spending, saving, and giving).  Within the budget, there should be a reflection of your goals as well.  You have to find your middle and your balance financially, which we will talk about, and reflect this in your budget.  From that point on, your budget becomes your reference point.  If you take your eyes off of the budget or worse, don't do a budget, you will not have a reference point and therefore be unbalanced and constantly falling.

❖ **Step 2** – The tightrope walker must keep making constant corrections as he is going across to the other side.  If you watch closely, you will see they are always moving slightly left or right.  If he doesn't make these constant corrections, he will stay unbalanced and fall.

In your finances, you are always making corrections, whether you realize it or not. Many times these corrections or changes are impulsive and damaging. In order to maintain balance, you need to keep your reference point of the budget always in sight and make constant corrections and adjustments to it as you go along. You will never have the same budget two months in a row and you will most likely have to change your monthly budget several times during the course of the month. This is an okay and necessary practice to implement. If you do a budget and then never adjust it as changes come up, you will find yourself out of balance at the end of the month. This will frustrate you and cause you to give up and fall down. You must always be aware of every dollar coming in and going out and always be making changes in order to stay balanced financially.

❖ **Step 3 –** A tightrope walker must always have a clear objective. His objective is always to get to the other side without falling down. He must always keep his objective clear in his mind and work, using steps 1 and 2, to meet that objective.

In your finances, you must also have a clear objective. The simplest, yet most important, objective to have is to maintain balance between working, spending, saving, and giving. If you don't know what your objectives are, you will just be out there, like a fish out of water, and look up in 5 years and be exactly where you were 5 years before, or worse, be worse off than you were 5 years before. Decide what your objectives are and write them down. Then look at them constantly and make corrections when necessary. Know where you are going.

### *Law of Pinocchio*

I heard this saying one time in a study on consequences. It is the perfect description of how to look at the personal finance world. The personal finance world does not work on the Laws of Pinocchio but on the Laws of Harvest. What does this mean?

Every time Pinocchio told a lie, his nose grew. There was an immediate consequence to his action. If there was an immediate consequence to our actions, we would become more cautious about the decisions and choices that we make. In personal finance, most of the consequences are not immediate. Therefore, it is hard for us to relate the consequences to the appropriate action. The best example of this is the housing crisis a few years ago. From 2003 to 2006, there was a boom of sub prime mortgages being issued. These mortgages were given at adjustable interest rates and usually with no money down. These loans were designed to prey on the people who wanted to own a home, but couldn't financially afford to own a home. The people who took out these mortgages did not feel the consequences of their bad decisions right away. It wasn't until 2008-2010 that the consequences of these loans were truly felt. At this time, people's rates began to adjust and the value of their homes dropped and the payments became unmanageable. They couldn't refinance because they weren't qualified plus their homes were underwater. This caused many people to lose their homes.

The housing crisis and economic issues of the last few years is a prime example of the Law of Harvest. Or in simple terms, you reap what you sow. Two farmers go through the time of sowing. It isn't until harvest time that you see the results of that sowing. It is only at the time of harvest that you see how wisely or how foolishly the farmer planted for the harvest. Immediately after sowing, the fields look the same. It is only with time and care that you begin to see which farmer sowed better. Two couples bought a house in 2005. One couple bought a $250,000 home with 20% down and a 6% fixed interest rate. The other couple bought a $250,000 home with no money down and a 9% adjustable interest rate. For the first couple of years, you wouldn't notice any difference in these two couples. As a matter of fact, couple number two probably had a lower monthly payment because many of the sub prime loans started out as interest only. But then the harvest came. The rate adjusted and couple number two's world came crashing down. They lost everything and had to start over.

Part of having balance in your financial life is finding the wise middle of decision making. For couple number two, they went to an extreme out of impatience and ignorance. Most people knew deep down these sub prime loans were too good to be true, but they wanted a house so bad they lost their balance. This is why I work so hard to teach balance in every area. For couple number two, balance would have been to rent very cheap and save like crazy to get at least 10% down if not 20%. Many people had to choose sub prime loans because of their credit. If you pay your bills on time and don't go into further debt, you can clean up your credit. Also, they could have researched and found a mortgage company to do manual underwriting. There is always a balanced solution to get anything you want. But you have to be wise enough and patient enough to find it and work toward it.

I wish the personal finance world worked through the Laws of Pinocchio because it would have saved me a lot of pain and heartache and probably you as well. But it doesn't. We have to realize that the decisions we are making today will have an impact on our future. Every dress you charge on a credit card affects your future. Every car you drive and how you pay for it affects your future. When you are making decisions, decide what you want your harvest to look like and make sure you are sowing the right seeds to produce it.

### *You Are Fired*

If you were a money manager and handled someone else's finances the way you handle your finances, would you keep your job or would you be fired? I'm afraid many of us would be fired. The reality is that you are a money manager. In 1 Chronicles 29:10-14, David prayed to God thanking him for his blessings, realizing that all of his wealth came from God. If you are a person of faith, don't believe that just because you give your obligatory 10% tithe that you can do what you want with the other 90%. Everything we have comes from God; therefore, the decisions we make about our money should honor God. Does it honor God to spend money on stuff you won't ever use, even if you can afford it? Does it honor God to waste money and stuff? When someone borrows something of yours, do you expect them to honor 60 or 70% of the item or 100% of the item? Of course, 100% and that is what God expects us to do with what he gives to us to manage.

If you are not a person of faith, you are still a money manager. You may not believe everything you own is God's but you can still be "fired" for not managing what you have well. The consequence of not managing what you have well is losing what you have. Have you ever looked up and wondered where your money went or why you are struggling so much financially? The first place to start looking is at your spending. It is more important to do a spending journal than it is a budget. You have to know where your money goes. Andy Stanley once said "You've got to be knowing where your money is going." You have to become a spy when it comes to your money.

Have you ever heard of a story where a wealthy person became broke? Of course you have. And I'm sure you said "If I had that much money, that would never happen to me." But it could happen to you just as quickly as it happened to them. It happened to them, most likely, because they were out of balance and not managing their money very well. You cannot have balance if you have no clue about each dollar you are spending. You can look up, as I did many times, and see what you made for the year and wonder what you have to show for it.

Start today by firing the old you. Then, hire the new you. The new you is very detail oriented. The new you will pay attention to every dollar coming in and every dollar going out. The new you will find a balance between working, spending, saving and giving by doing a fair amount of each. The new you will show more profit than ever before and turn your financial situation around.

The more money you have, the more out of balance you can get. It is easy to manage our money when we don't have a lot. But the more we get, the more we spend and the more we stop paying attention. I challenge you today to start paying attention. Begin to handle your finances as if you were handling them for someone else. Keep in balance everyday and watch how much more money you will have. It works because I've done it.

# P is for Perspective

*Y*our perspective is very simple. It is how you look at things or how you interpret a situation. Let me give you an example and see what your perspective would be. This is a letter written by a college student to her parents.

*Dear Mom and Dad,*

*I am doing well. My cuts and bruises are finally healing from having to jump out of my dorm window during the fire. But don't worry. There was a nice young man there to take care of me when I fell. Since I had no where to live, he is letting me stay with him. I can't wait for you to meet him. I know that you will welcome him with open arms even though he is of a different race and religion than you are. I hope you can meet him soon, before the baby is born. That's right; you are going to be grandparents. I know you can't wait.*

*Don't worry mom and dad. There was no fire. I am not living with a man and I am not pregnant.*

*However, I do have a D in English and Chemistry. I can't wait to see you.*

The student wrote the letter this way to put her situation into perspective for her parents. Her parents, like most, would have gotten upset over the bad grades. But when the bad grades were put into perspective of what life could look like, it was much easier for the parents to accept the grades.

What kind of perspective do you have of your personal finances? Do you realize that what you have going on right now may be stressful, but could be worse? Or do you believe that this situation is so bad you will never recover and nobody has it as bad as you do? Have you ever seen the television show "Extreme Home Makeover"? If you really want to put your life into perspective, you should watch it sometime. I saw a show one time where a couple with six kids didn't have running water. First, I thought about how a family living in the United States could not have running water. Then, I became very thankful for my life and my running water.

You cannot have a positive life and negative thoughts. If you are always losing perspective and getting stressed out over every little thing, you will have trouble having a positive life. Did you realize that to many people, in the U.S. and abroad, you are wealthy? You may not consider yourself that way, but you are very blessed. We think we are not wealthy because we cannot buy what we want to buy or because we live paycheck to paycheck. But most of us live that way by choice because we choose to go into debt to obtain more stuff. Let's see if you are wealthy or not.

- ❖ Do you own two cars or more?
- ❖ Do you have more than two pairs of shoes?
- ❖ Do you have more than three outfits?
- ❖ Do you have a winter coat?
- ❖ Do you eat three meals a day?
- ❖ Do you have running, hot water?

These are just a few of the basics not to mention all of the extras we have such as cable, cell phones, computers, multiple televisions and more. We need to take a moment and put our true financial situation into the right perspective. Your life is a movie not a picture. You do not have to stay where you are today. Your story is ongoing and you have the ability to change your story as you see fit. A large part of your story is your perspective.

## *To Worry or Not To Worry*

When something unexpected happens in your financial life, is your perspective or outlook negative or positive? Do you automatically jump to the negative no matter what the unexpected thing is, just like the parents in our story? This constant negativity will only lead to constant worry and worry leads to nowhere. There is no button to turn worry off, but changing your perspective about your situations can remove the worry from your thoughts. First of all, we have to realize that 80% of what we worry about never happens. Most of the 20% left that does happen we have no control over. So why spend your life, as short as it is, worrying. Do you know how many people file bankruptcy on what might happen? Sometimes it is necessary to file bankruptcy. It was for me, but you should never file based on what you think is going to happen in the future. Only file if, and when, it becomes the only option for you.

We spend too much of our time dreading the next thing. We miss the joy of the current events worrying about the next thing that could happen. Perhaps you get a raise at work, but you are too worried about your debt and paying this month's bills to take in the blessing of the extra income. Or maybe you miss a great sermon on Sunday morning, which you really could use, because all you can think about is the traffic leaving and how much housework you have to do. We also spend a lot of our time playing the "I'll be happy when..." game. If you are playing this game, you will miss out on the current joys in your life. Happiness cannot be bought. Happiness comes from joy and enjoying life as it goes. Worry will steal your happiness.

This happens a lot in the arena of our kids. We are so busy worrying about them and what they are going to become that we forget to enjoy them. We need to find our hope and our joy and ditch our worry. There are steps you can take financially to decrease the worry factor in your life. My life story is a great example of this. I spent many years of my life constantly worrying. I dreaded going to work everyday because I was working just to pay my bills. I was always worried about getting fired even though I wasn't doing anything that should get me fired. Everyday I hated to get home and check the mail. I was always worried about what was in the mailbox. I was afraid every time I used a credit card or debit card, wondering if it would be approved. I hated when the phone rang and would get a knot in my stomach every time it did. I was constantly worried I was hearing noises with my car when I was driving it. I spent so many years worrying about every little thing that several years of my life are a blur.

As I begin to change my financial life, my worry factor began to decrease. As my debts decreased and began to get paid off, I didn't worry as much about the mailbox, the phone, or my job. As I saved up an emergency fund, I worried less about the noises in the car and whether or not my debit card would be approved. I will never forget the first day I walked proudly to the mailbox knowing that I was on the right track financially, finally.

That is what true freedom is. That is what true happiness is. Being able to enjoy life without worry. Sure, inconveniences are going to happen. Life is going to happen. But your positive perspective and outlook on these inconveniences will change your life.

### *Your Outlook*

What is your outlook on your current financial situation and your future financial situation? Do you see a positive future for yourself or do you have trouble looking past today? You can never let your future be determined by your past. We have all made mistakes and we all have regrets about our past. But your past has made you who you are and who you are going to be. If I let my past determine my future, I would not be where I am today. I have many regrets, but I never spend time on them because I have realized that without going through everything that I have gone through, I would not be where I am. And I would not have the knowledge that I have to be able to help other people everyday to not have to go through what I went through. Let your mistakes become your message. That is the only thing that makes them worth it. I am always sharing my mistakes with my daughter and am always brutally honest about them because if I can prevent her from making the same mistakes as me, it is worth everything I went through. This is not only in the area of finance, but in relationships, school, and boys.

Many of us find ourselves at a point where the only thing we can do is start over. Colonel Sanders started over at 65 building Kentucky Fried Chicken. Your life doesn't have to be over just because you lost everything, or what you thought was everything. Life will never turn out how you planned for it to. Sometimes it will be better and sometimes it will be worse. But how you move through life, your story, is completely up to you. When you are faced with the challenge of starting over, treat your finances like a puzzle.

- ❖ Lay out the pieces
- ❖ Establish your borders
- ❖ Never force pieces that just don't fit
- ❖ Do a little at a time

Once you do these steps, your picture will come together. This can work in any part of your life where you have to start over.

You have to stop trying to figure everything out and find peace in not always knowing what the future holds. You are the only author of your story, nobody else. Remember, your story is a movie, an ongoing saga, not a picture, a frozen moment in time. Your perspective is one of the stars of your movie. How you look at your past, your present and your future is a key element to the script of your movie. There will be pain in your life. If your perspective is right, the end will always be worth the pain.

# Q is for Questions

*Q*uestions are always important. And, as you have probably heard, there are never any stupid questions. Without questions, we would never have answers and we would go through life just guessing. But we need to know what questions to ask in order to get the answers that we need. In personal finance, the questions can be as simple as who, what, when, where and why. This chapter is going to help you answer those questions in order to get you started on a path to decide other questions that need to be asked so that you can get the proper, wise answers you need in dealing with the everyday decisions of personal finance.

### Why?

This is usually the last question asked, but for you it needs to be the first question asked. It is necessary for us to know why we are doing something or we will never do it. This is imperative when it comes to your personal finances. If you don't know why you should do something, you will never do it and the other four questions really won't matter.  Without the why there will be no who, what, when or where.

- ❖ Why should you get out of debt?
- ❖ Why should you pay cash for everything, including cars and houses?
- ❖ Why should you budget?
- ❖ Why should you keep track of every purchase you make and every dollar you make?
- ❖ Why should you never lend money or cosign for someone?
- ❖ Why should you save 15% to 18% for retirement from age 25 to 65?

Many people are afraid to ask these questions because the real answer, the wise answer, scares them.  The answer means that they will have to be disciplined, that they will have to say no to themselves and others sometimes, and they will have to pay close attention to what is going on.

Let's take one of the above questions and analyze all sides of it and see what we can come up with.  You know you don't like the state of your finances right now and you know something needs to change. You read, in a previous chapter, that you should pay attention to every dollar, incoming and outgoing. This isn't something you have ever done or seen done. So, of course, you want to know why you should track every dollar coming in and going out in a spending journal. If you can't figure out why you should do it, you will never do it. So here is your why. The best way to control your money and have more money is to know what you have. You know, even if it is deep down, that you will never be wealthy if you spend more than you make. If you don't pay attention by tracking everything using Quicken, a note pad or a free internet website, you will wake up at the end of each year having no clue where your money went. And if you keep this up, you will look up 10 years from now, as many of you probably have, with nothing, still spending more than you make.

So, you know that what you have been doing isn't working. You hear a different way to handle your daily personal finances. You want to know why this way will work for you and why you should try it. I have explained why and it seems reasonable. So, now you can try it for a few months knowing the why. If someone just yells at you to pay attention to your money, you never will. Or if someone calls you stupid for not paying attention, you never will. You have to have a why.

I would be willing to bet that you hardly ever know the why of your decisions. Most people just do what everyone else is doing or they do something out of habit. It is important to start looking for your why. Look at a situation, lay all of your options out, and begin to make wise decisions based on the future, not just today. And then find your why. When your friends, family or society begin to criticize you because you went a different way, remember why you are doing it the wise way. Begin to find out why God put you here. We all have a purpose and a gift. Sometimes the whys are as simple as obeying God or as complicated as it is what is best for a future you can't even dream of yet. Dare to dream and use those whys to fulfill those dreams.

### *What?*

What do you need to do to get your financial life where you want it? What do you need to do to make your financial dreams come true? What do you need to do to have peace financially and live a life without financial stress? The answers to these questions are going to be different for everyone. Common sense, when it comes to personal finance, is pretty much the same but personal finance itself is just that, personal. You have to have dreams and goals in your personal finance or you will stay where you are.

Here is an example from my own life. I did almost everything wrong, financially speaking, for several years after I graduated college. I had no solid financial dreams and goals. I wanted to be comfortable, financially, and to be able to buy what I wanted. That was it. And that attitude got me in a lot of trouble. When I hit my bottom, and filed for bankruptcy, I decided that what I had been doing obviously was wrong, but I still didn't know what was right. I had done wrong for so long I couldn't see the right way to handle my finances. So, I began to search for the right way. I used the Bible, I read books like this, and I began to look at the examples of the right way (i.e. my parents and some family) to find the answers.

At that point, I began to figure out my dreams and financial goals that I wanted for myself (my why). The next step was to figure out what I needed to do to reach those dreams and goals. I had to decide what was best for me and based on who I was, what I needed to change to get there. As I have said before, personal finance is very personal. Everyone is different and will find peace in different ways. There are people who can use credit cards and pay them off every month. There are people who can take out a car loan, and choose to because they will pay less in interest than they would make on their cash, and pay it off in 2 to 3 years instead of 5 years. But I was not one of those people.

What I needed to do to find peace was have an emergency fund, get out of debt, start paying close attention to my money, and learning to say no to myself. The biggest step I had to take was to find contentment in what I had and become a replacer and not an upgrader. At this point, I knew what I needed to do to make my goals a reality. My goals are always changing and my what has to change with it. Ask yourself today what you need to do in order to reach peace in your personal finances.

### *When?*

When is very simple, now! "Never put off until tomorrow what you can do today." We have talked a lot about looking up in five years and being exactly where you were five years before. Remember the "I'll be happy when…" game from the last chapter. You need to be happy now. You need to find happiness in your circumstances, whatever they are. In the "I'll be happy when…" game, when never comes. For example, you say you'll be happier when you get a bigger house. The house you have right now is way too small. But when you get the bigger house, there is more house to clean, more yard to mow and more mortgage and taxes to pay. Odds are you will not be happier in the bigger house. The only thing that will change is what you are unhappy about. In the first house it was not enough space and in this house it will be what happens when you have more space.

There is no better time than now to start on a new financial path, one that leads to peace and freedom. Why would you wait a year to start getting out of debt? Why would you wait to begin investing for your retirement? Why would you wait a year or two to begin the steps to a career in a field that you are passionate about? Why would you wait to start walking down your new path?

There are sometimes emotional obstacles that get in our way and delay our now. But you have to find the strength to overcome these emotions and start today.

Fear is a huge obstacle.  Fear will never go away, but it is okay to do it afraid.  I have done many things in my life afraid.  If I had waited for the fear to go away, I would have wasted valuable time and maybe even missed a great opportunity.  Another huge obstacle is self esteem. Many people do not have the confidence in themselves to make the changes they want to make.  You can do it and especially if it is an area that is passionate to you because odds are that is a calling on your life.  Sometimes you have to go for it.  You will make mistakes, but you adjust and keep going.  Never giving up is how winners win.

Unfortunately, selfishness can also play a factor emotionally in starting down your new path.  If you begin today to get out of debt or change careers, you are going to have to make sacrifices and this means saying no to yourself.

I hope that you will decide today to start down your new financial path, whatever that looks like in your world. There will always be obstacles out there getting in your way and you have to decide how important your new path is to your happiness and your peace.  Take it from someone who has been there.  It is hard and painful at times.  It takes a lot of courage, courage that I didn't think I had.  But I decided that giving up was not an option.  I went through some hard times, but life is easier now.  You can pick hard now and easy later or easy now and hard later.  I would much rather have a little hard now and a lot of easy later on than I would really easy now and very hard later on.  The choice is yours.  Choose now!

### *Where?*

Where, in this instance, isn't geographical.  It is categorical.  Where, in what areas, do you need to make some changes in your financial life?  Do you need to change some bad habits you have, maybe even without knowledge, formed over the years?  Do you need to basically change everything you are doing because nothing is working?  Or do you just need to focus more on a category or two, such as your investing and retirement.  The where is, like everything else in personal finance, different for everyone.

A great place to answer the question of where is in your spending plan.  Hopefully, after contemplating the why, what and when so far, you have decided to begin a spending plan if you don't already have one in place.

Within your spending plan is a great place for the where question. Where can we either increase our income or cut our expenses? Here are a few examples of each and we will cover more in a couple of chapters from now.

- ❖ Is there overtime or extra work that I can do to increase my income?
- ❖ Is there anything I can sell to give us some extra money toward our goals?
- ❖ Is there a special with my cable provider to get all of my services for a deal, locked in for at least a year or two?
- ❖ Are there any features we have on our cell phone bill that we can eliminate to lower our payment?
- ❖ Are there any discount grocery stores in our town where I can get the same food for lower prices?
- ❖ Are we in a position to set our automobile insurance deductible at $1000 to lower our monthly payment?

You really should look at every category on your spending plan and address each one. I found, when I was looking to quit my job and work from home full time, that every category in my budget could be adjusted. I was able to lower almost every item to live within the boundaries of my husband's income. I actually found it a challenge, and a little like a game after a while, to spend as little money as I could per month and save and give as much as I could.

I hope that you will take the time to be honest and discover where you need to make some changes in order to make the most of your financial life and bring yourself peace in your finances.

### *Who?*

Who is responsible for your actions? Who is responsible for your financial situation? Who is going to change your financial situation? The answer to all of these questions is you. Until you accept responsibility for where you are and understand that you are the only one that can change it, your situation will only get worse. I ask clients all the time what happened to get them to where they are today, financially. And very rarely does anyone ever say to me, "Debbi, I just screwed up and I want to change that." Many people even come to me hoping for a magic formula to fix everything for them because that is easier than accepting responsibility. Another game that we love to play is the blame game. It is so much easier to blame someone else for our situation. If you have lost your job lately, do you blame the economy for your financial troubles? Is it possible that your biggest financial problem is not that you lost your job, but that you didn't have 6-8 months worth of expenses saved in an emergency fund? That isn't the economy's fault. That is yours, most likely caused by living beyond your means.

I had a client once whose husband had left her and filed for divorce. First of all, she blamed him for everything even though she had treated him disrespectfully for 20 years. I am not saying he handled it correctly, because he didn't, but she needed to take responsibility for her part as well. Then she was given the house by her ex husband and was awarded alimony for 8 years, the law in her state. During those 8 years, she only worked part time and relied solely on her alimony to pay her bills. Even then, it wasn't enough. But somehow, she was shocked when the alimony stopped and she had to support herself. She had 8 years that she could have been working full time, paying off her debt, saving and setting up her lifestyle for when the alimony ended. There are many single women out there making it just fine on a full time income. But instead of taking responsibility for her own life and her financial circumstances, it was easier for her to blame her ex-husband. How different her life would be now if she had just accepted responsibility for her life and stopped blaming other people for her financial situation.

We have to stop blaming (the economy, the government, and other people) and stop looking to everyone else to solve our problems (the economy, the government, and other people). There will never be a government program that will solve your financial problems. Truthfully, they usually make them worse. Once you realize that you are in control of your financial life and that you can decide what it is going to look like, you can begin to make progress. You are the author of your story. Who is responsible for your situation? You are. Who is going to change your situation and make it awesome? You are.

We need to always be asking questions and through those questions, gain answers and knowledge. Why, what, when, where, and who are questions to get you started. They are the most important questions because they involve your financial life in a personal and intimate way. They also require truth which is a valuable tool for wealth. Never stop asking questions.

> *Successful people ask better questions, and as a result, they get better answers.*
>
> Tony Robbins

# R is for the Road to Recovery

*I* want you, right now, to take everything you have and move to Recovery Street. This is an awesome street to live on. There are houses that people can afford to buy, there are paid for cars in the driveways, there are shops to purchase your needs, and there is family. I know that right now this country needs to begin their journey on the road to recovery, but I imagine you do as well. The road to recovery begins with you and hopefully other people will follow and in turn, our country will recover as well.

### What is the problem?

I hardly ever talk politics in what I do and I won't start today. However, it is necessary to be honest about the financial state of our union. In our country, we do not have a prosperity problem. We have an abuse of prosperity problem. We also do not have a cash flow problem. We have a spending problem. We cannot continue to ignore these problems. The tendency of people is to ignore a problem until it becomes a financial problem. For instance, many people do not realize they have a drug abuse problem until it affects them financially and then it can be too late. There is more than enough money in this country to provide for the needs of the people and to run this country. There is more than likely enough money in your household to take care of you and your family. However, there are a few problems, such as the abuse of prosperity and the spending problems that creep in and take over. It is only when these problems hit us financially, as they are doing now, that we wake up and pay attention. We need to pay attention at all times in order to avoid these problems altogether. There are also a few other problems that have begun to creep in over the last several decades that are causing major financial issues and if we don't eliminate these problems, we will continue on the current financial path we are on and never get on the road to recovery.

❖ **A Discipline Problem** – We have a major discipline problem in this country. We have no clue how to say NO! If a group of people complains and whines enough, the government sets up a program for them. In most cases, these programs and money just continue to enable the people to live in their problems and not to solve them. We are constantly reaching into our futures to solve today's problems because we do not have the discipline and patience we need to solve our problems currently. You cannot keep mortgaging your future, as a country or as an individual, and not have it catch up to you at some point, in a very uncomfortable way. When you have more than you need, you are never disciplined and that is our true state of the union.

❖ **An Entitlement Problem** – Having a sense of entitlement means you owe me something. I can have what I want just because I want it. There is one word that best describes this attitude – spoiled. We used to find spoiled people only among the wealthy. They had the ability, financially, to have anything they desired and their attitude reflected that. But today, in the world of debt, almost everyone has a sense of entitlement. There are people who won't buy a house just because the kitchen or the bathroom isn't updated to the modern styles out there. They can't see past buying the house because it is the best deal and then making cosmetic changes as they go along. They want it their way before they will even consider buying it. Every kid I knows expects to get a cell phone when they turn 10 years old. It is as if they can't live without them. But they can and they should. Parents are teaching their kids to feel entitled and it is going to keep getting worse as time goes on. No one owes you anything and it is possible, even probable, that you will have to work, save, and wait to get what you want. If you get everything you want just because you want it, you are spoiled and adding to the state of the union.

❖ **A Greed Problem** – Greed is a major problem in this country and it is an attitude of greed that has caused most of the problems we are currently facing. Greed means that if it is in my hands, it is mine. Greed is also having the mindset that you are going to have money at whatever the cost. Did you know that the more money you make, the less, percentage wise, you are liable to give away? Wealthy people may give away more dollars per year, but the percentage of their giving is much less than your average person. But in recent years, the average person has also been giving less. The national average for giving is 3%-5%. This includes people of the Christian faith who are taught to give 10%. We have more money than ever in this country, but we are keeping it all for ourselves. If you do not have a giving heart, you will never be wealthy. If you are keeping all of your money and not giving some of it away, you are contributing to the state of the union.

❖ **A Coward Problem** – Or as a friend of mine put it once, a failure of nerve problem. We see the problem and we see the solution. But we choose to do nothing about it. If you are a parent, have you ever been afraid to tell you child no? Do you think it is just easier to give them everything they want and then you don't have to hear it? If this is the case, you have a coward problem. You are letting your kids control your life. All of us pout and sulk when we don't get our way and especially teenagers and young adults. But it is our job as parents to teach our kids the meaning of the word no. I have found myself in this position many times because I say no a lot. But I have always found that after the initial pout, sulking and eye rolling and after my explanation, my daughter usually will accept what my decisions are. We have to stick to what we know is right and wise and not what the world is doing. If you are running your financial world the way the rest of the country is doing it, you are contributing to the state of the union.

Have you ever heard of a millionaire filing for bankruptcy and you said "If I had that kind of money, that would never happen to me."?  Have you ever heard of a major company going out of business or filing for bankruptcy and you said "That would never happen on my watch."?  You believe that you are much smarter and this would never happen if you were in their position or in charge.  But what do your finances look like?  Would someone else look at your finances and disagree with you?  We never know what happened in these scenarios and we don't know that we would be able to do any better.  Most of the time, it is one, or maybe all, of the above problems that have caused the issue.  I challenge you to take a look at your finances and see if they reflect any or all of the above problems.  And if they do, decide today that you are going to be a solution in the state of our union and not part of the problem.  Recovery has to start on an individual level first and it will then spread higher and higher until we are able to see the recovery this country needs so desperately.

### *It all begins with you!*

You would never be wrong on purpose. But that doesn't change the fact that many of the decisions people are making are wrong and in many cases very wrong. We will always reap what we sow and we are doing that as a nation and as individuals right now. You have to begin your own individual road to recovery first. You have to look at yourself first and not at everyone else. You can't change other people, ever, not even a child or a spouse. But you can change you and hope that that change influences other people along the way. Matthew 7:3-5 is a perfect example of this. Jesus says that you must first take the plank out of your eye before you can remove the speck from someone else's eye. We are so busy telling each other what other people or our government is doing wrong in their finances that we forget to look at what we are doing wrong in our finances. We must look in the mirror first and remove our plank, change what we are doing wrong, before we can even think of criticizing someone else for what we think they are doing wrong.

The recovery of the state of the union, financially speaking, begins with we not they, me not you. Let's look at a few areas of your decision making that you may be able to change in a positive way to aide in your recovery.

* ❖ How do your handle your money?  Are you living below your means or do you spend every penny you have?  If you are in debt and always spending more than you make, how can you criticize the government for doing the same thing?  Begin today to develop a plan for getting out of debt, living within your means, and saving for emergencies and for the future.

* ❖ Are you greedy with your money?  For example, is 98% of your money spent on lifestyle and the other 2% on others?  What percentage of your money do you give away?  If you never give anything away, how can you criticize the government for supporting corporations where greed runs amuck?  Begin today to work into your budget at least 10% of your income to go to other people, whatever form that takes on for you.

* ❖ Are you on disability but you are able to do work of some kind?  I am not talking to the people with true disabilities.  I am talking to the people who just

don't want to work and rely on the government to take care of them. If you are collecting disability but are able to answer a phone, you are not disabled and you should be working. How can you criticize the government for all of the money they spend supporting people who are disabled when you are using the system? Begin today to think of something you can do, even with your disability, and make yourself proud. If you know of someone abusing the system, instead of criticizing them, help them to be confident and to find something they are good at.

These are just a few examples of things that you may be doing, even without realizing it, that you can examine during your recovery journey. Make sure that you are living a life of true integrity and not with an attitude of everybody owes me. Do you take supplies home with you from work? Do you use the internet at work even though it is against policy? When you drop something on the floor when you are shopping, do you pick it up? When you go to the movies, do you throw away your trash? You can't excuse wrong or lazy behavior by using the line "that is what they get paid for" or "they owe me for everything I give." Remember change in this country is going to begin with you.

We have American problems, not party problems. However, these problems, along with our attitudes, have caused party problems. I remember when a Democrat and a Republican could sit on the porch, drink a glass of sweet tea, and discuss their opinions and differences without argument. That is not the case today. You must remember that everyone has an opinion and they are just as entitled to it as you are. In most cases, no one is 100% correct anyway. There are two sides to every pancake.

Mature people don't look for someone to blame. They look for solutions. I want you to become a part of the solution, not the problem. Whatever recovery looks like in your financial world, you need to begin your journey today. You are the answer. When you begin to write your story, other people will follow. The recovery of this nation is not going to start in Washington D.C. It is going to start in your home. It has to start with you or it will never get better. Make the decision today to be the answer this country needs. Be the solution, not the problem.

*Do not be deceived: God cannot be mocked. A man reaps what he sows. Whoever sows to please their flesh, from the flesh will reap destruction; whoever sows to please the Spirit, from the Spirit will reap eternal life.*

*Galatians 6:7-8*

# S is for Spending Plan

*A* spending plan, a.k.a. a budget, is the best tool you can use to obtain wealth and find peace, financially speaking. There is no way you would ever build a house without very detailed plans. If you did, it would fall down around you and bury you. Your finances follow the same guidelines. If you do not have detailed plans regarding your money, your financial world will fall down around you and bury you. You have to be in control of your money and tell it where you want it to go every month and with every dollar. A lot of people are currently spending more than they make per month and the main reason isn't debt, although that is a major problem, but it is because they do not have any control over their money. They just keep spending and spending and look up one day and it is gone. Then they have to use debt to take care of their needs until they can catch up. The cycle keeps repeating itself; therefore, they will never catch up. I will state the obvious again to you. You will never have any money if you keep spending more than you make.

You cannot use credit cards to live on when you retire. You need cash and the best way to have that cash is to spend less than you make and invest the difference.

### *The Spending Journal*

People who have never done a budget before usually have trouble with where to start and all get it wrong for the first few months, even if they are math and detail oriented. We will talk about how to lay out a budget in a few minutes which is simple since it is basically third grade math. The hard part is the emotional part that comes with doing a budget. Most people have in their head what they would like to spend in different categories, but their reality is very different from their head.

The best first step of the budgeting process is to do a spending journal for at least three months. This is a tool that you should continue to use in conjunction with a budget, but for now the purpose is for you to get a grip on your reality. All you need is a piece of paper and a pencil (or you can use software on your computer, if you wish). For every dollar you spend you write down the date, where and what you spent the money on, and how much it was. As I have said before, you have to stand in your truth in order to prosper. A spending journal is a picture of your truth. A spending journal will not only tell you how much you are spending but will show you where you can cut some of your spending in order to find more cash. Everyone I have ever known who has started a budget and used a spending journal has always found extra cash after the first few months.

You should not start a budget until you have done a spending journal for at least 3 months. Once you have, you can begin the process of laying out an accurate and realistic budget for your money. There will always be times where your budget will have to be adjusted, probably at least once a month, but the adjustments need to be due to unforeseen items, not because you don't know what you are spending. Once you start your budget, you still should continue with a spending journal because it is imperative to know where your money is going and how you and your spouse are spending it. A budget and a spending journal are both great marriage communication tools. Many marriages have been saved just by implementing these two items into their financial world. When everything is laid out, there are no secrets and financial secrets are the number one cause for divorce. You want a happy and successful marriage; begin to use a budget and spending journal today.

### *The Dreaded "B" Word*

A budget is not a controlling device. It is a communication tool, communication between you and your money and communication between you and your spouse. We have talked about before how personal finance is 10% math and 90% emotion. A budget is the area where these percentages show up the most. A budget, mathematically speaking, is third grade math. But the emotions that go into the decisions of a budget are much harder. A budget is a reflection of your priorities and goals in life. You have taken a huge step toward financial maturity just by doing a budget. Discipline is the primary ingredient in budgeting. Discipline is planning your pain and your pleasure and a budget or spending plan is the best tool for this.

A budget has to be put down on paper and must reflect the entire month, month by month. The reason this is important is because if you do a budget paycheck to paycheck, you will miss items and always come up short at the end of the month. I had a client who was a great example of this. She and her ex husband each contributed to their daughter's lunch account. She would add money for two weeks and he would add money two weeks later and they alternated this way. Well, she always budgeted for the lunch money in her monthly budget so when it came time for her to add the money to the account, she was ready. However, her ex wasn't quite as efficient so when the money ran out and it was his turn to add it, it came as a surprise and messed up his "paycheck budget". I actually do a monthly budget, which contains all of my bills for the month and then a paycheck budget, which takes the monthly budget and breaks it down by paycheck so I make sure every dollar out of every paycheck is distributed where it needs to go.

There are many ways to do a budget, but I am going to explain the simple way and you can tech it up it you want to. You simply need to take out a piece of paper, write down your income for the month at the top and then write down every bill you have going down the page. I always write my fixed expenses, expenses that never change such as mortgage, insurance, cable, etc., together and then my controllable expenses, expenses that may change or be adjusted each month, together. Then you simply subtract your expenses from your income. See how simple that is. Now comes the hard part.

You want to work on what I refer to as a zero dollar budget. This means that you want every dollar you are going to make to go somewhere, including savings, college, investing, financial goals, etc. You want every dollar in a spending category so that there is no mystery as to where it is going. If you tell it where to go, then you are in control and you are the only one who can change where it goes. Most months you are going to have "surprise" expenses come up. You can either take from one category to cover the "surprise" or you can budget what I call a G.O.K (God Only Knows) category. This can just be a few dollars that will cover the "surprises" and can be carried over from month to month if not used. If you end up with a negative budget, then you have two choices. You can either bring in more income through part time jobs or selling stuff or you will have to prioritize your expenses and someone will not get paid. Let me give you a hint about this part – it will not be your mortgage or car not getting paid, it will be a credit card. And yes they will yell and they will call, but you have to prioritize correctly and pay for your main needs first and always (lights, food, shelter, and transportation).

I could write an entire book on budgeting, covering in detail the math and the emotions. Therefore, I am not able to cover everything in this one chapter. But here are the most important things to know about budgeting and doing a spending plan.

❖ It is imperative that you do one. You will never have extra until you control where your money is going. You must be in control of your money.

❖ I recommend doing a monthly and a paycheck budget. There is a sample in your workbook of the one that I use that will help you tremendously. You need to lay out your entire month and then distribute your paychecks accordingly.

❖ You have to make sure that all of the elements of personal finance are included in your budget - work, spend, save, and give - as well as your financial goals. Most people use the order of spend, save, and give. Try flipping your order to give, save, and spend. The formula and numbers are usually the same, but your attitude will change for the better.

❖ If you are married, you must do the budget together, even if that means one of you writes it all out and does the math and then shows it to the other.  Both of you must have a vote and a voice in where the money goes.  And if the budget needs to change during the month, you need to come back together to decide where the changes will be made.  Schedule at least one monthly budget meeting during the last week of each month to develop and go over the next month's budget and call mini meetings when "surprises" come up.  Use a budget as the marriage saving tool it is known to be.

You are never too wealthy to do a budget.  You must always know where your money is going.  If you were CEO of a major company, you would never say "We have so much money, we don't need to keep track anymore."  You would be broke within months.  We are stewards of God's money and all that he has blessed us with.  Show Him how thankful you are by paying attention.  I was once told that there are two types of people in this world; those who make interest and those who pay interest.  Be a person who makes interest because you are paying attention, not one who pays interest because you use debt to solve your disorganization.  If you keep doing the same thing, not using a spending plan, and expect different results, you are insane according to Einstein.  I know you are not insane and I believe that you are going to give this spending plan and spending journal a try.

### *The Savings Game*

I wanted to write this last part to help you in your journey to using a budget and saving money everywhere you can. I have mentioned some of these in a previous chapter but I want to cover them in the context of your budget. You need to always be finding the least expensive way to meet your needs and get your wants. Do you know how most people become millionaires? It is not by inheriting millions or running mega companies. It is by always working hard, spending less than they make, having a charitable heart, and saving every penny they can. Don't think yourself too entitled or above doing some or all of the suggestions below.

❖ Shop for clothing, shoes, purses, books, etc. in good quality thrift stores such as the Salvation Army. Make sure you keep an eye out for their specials. For example, Wednesday's here are ½ off day. So I always take my teenage daughter there on Wednesdays and she usually finds really nice, name brand clothes in good shape.

❖ Look for the discount grocery stores in your area. Most food is the same whether is has a brand name label or not. For example, we have an Aldi's here and I do a lot of my shopping there. The condiments, meat, eggs, milk, etc are the same as in the big grocery stores for a much less price. Don't get me wrong; I still buy name brand on some things. For instance, I buy name brand potato chips. But don't be afraid to try things and see, especially on expensive items like cereal, meats, etc.

❖ Don't drive all around town trying to save 3 cents on gasoline. If you have a 16 gallon tank, you are only saving 48 cents and you will spend more than that driving around. Find ways to save gas money in other areas. Make sure you get regular oil changes, change your air filter regularly, make sure your tire pressure is correct, and drive the speed limit. You may think these small things won't matter, but I started saving about 50 miles on a tank of gas. That's about 2 gallons which today is about $7.00. That is much better than 48 cents.

❖ Raise your automotive and home owners insurance deductibles up to $1000. If you have an issue, your emergency fund will cover the deductible and you will save a lot of money per year on your premium.

❖ Get the most you can out of your utilities. Put your electric and gas on a budget plan if possible. This won't save you money but will help you budget better. What will save you money is unplugging plugs that are not in use, adjusting your thermostat when you are not home, finding the best settings on your washer and dryer, combining hand washing and using the dishwasher, and turning off your computers and unplugging them when they are not in use. These are just a few of the many things I changed and lowered my bill by a lot.

❖ Get only what you can afford on cable, home phone, cell phones, and internet. You do not have to have hundreds of channels and every option they offer.  Set your budget and shop and negotiate accordingly.

Again, these are just a few of the things that I have done and that have worked for me, saving me hundreds per month and I wanted to share them with you.  I hope you will give them a try and that they will work for you too.

In this country, there are times when we are asked to give to help those less fortunate than us but we say we can't because we do not have the cash right now.  But when we want to buy something or spend money, we say "No problem, I'll just use credit."  A budget will help with both of these problems.  A budget will take what we make by working and distribute it for giving, saving, and spending and will help us to control those areas of our financial world.  A budget is a very important guardrail that everyone needs because without it you can run off your financial road very quickly and hurt yourself.  I want you to think of a budget as a positive, wise step for the very mature and wise person that I know you are.

> *"Suppose one of you wants to build a tower.*
> *Won't you first sit down and estimate the cost*
> *to see if you have enough money to complete it?*
> *Luke 14:28*

# T is for the Ten Commandments of Personal Finance

7he Ten Commandments are God's boundaries for us. As we have discussed before, boundaries or guardrails are vital to our lives. I believe that if you can follow these ten commandments of personal finance, you will establish great boundaries and you will prosper in your financial life.

I. **Thou shalt not use debt and credit cards.** Debt and credit cards are not the answer to solving your problems. Many generations before ours lived and survived without debt and credit cards. It has only been in the last 40 years or so, and much more in the last 20 years, that debt and credit cards have become the solution for every problem. These are socially acceptable sins, meaning that everyone knows that these are not the answer, but everyone is doing it, so that makes it okay. It does not. You should not buy anything you do not have the money for. It was good enough for our grandparents and it is good enough for us.

II. **Thou shalt only have a mortgage if the payment is less than 27% of your income and is on a 15 year fixed rate and you can put at least 20% down.** I would love for everyone to pay cash for their houses like our grandparents did, but I know that is not always possible. However, there is a way to get a house that will not end up bankrupting you in the future. First, it must be no more than 27% of your income. This is an amount you can pay comfortably even when life happens (loss of job, big emergency, etc). You need to put at least 20% down for 2 reasons. One is you won't need PMI and second is you will likely always have equity in your home. And if you get a 15 year fixed rate mortgage, you don't have to worry about the interest rate changing and you can have it paid off very quickly. Many Americans don't follow any of this commandment and are losing their homes left and right for one or all of the reasons above. Let a house be a blessing, not a curse.

III. **Thou shalt never co-sign or lend money to a friend or family member.** When a person needs a co-signer, it is because they cannot get a loan on their own. You cannot participate in their denial. They will always have good intentions and plan to pay it back, but the reality is that they probably can't. Then, you are not only liable for the money, but your relationship with this person will never be the same. This commandment includes student loans for your children. Children are not exempt from this commandment. We all love our children, but sometimes the best thing for our children is to say no. Also, do not lend family or anyone money for the same reasons. If you feel someone really needs the money and you can afford to give it to them then do so, but as a gift not a loan. "The borrower is slave to the lender."

IV. **Thou shalt always pay with cash.** This is both literally and figuratively. Paying with cash means you do not buy something you do not have the money to pay for right then. This means that if you want or need something, you save up for it and pay cash. You should also literally pay with cash whenever you can. Debit cards are great and I use them. However, there is proven research that it hurts a lot more to pay with cash than to swipe a card. When you only have $100 in your grocery envelope, you are only going to spend $100. If you use your debit card, you may spend $110 because you can, but $10 over time can add up very quickly.

V. **Thou shalt always budget and treat that budget like a contract.** You should do a written spending plan every month before the first day of the month. This doesn't need to be fancy. Just list your income for the month at the top of a page and decide where every dollar is going to go for the month. Make sure you pay necessities first and then you and your spouse decide where the other money is going. Once you decide, the spending plan becomes a contract and can only be changed with the consent of both of you. If you don't control your money and tell it where to go, I promise it will control you.

VI.  **Thou shalt always have an emergency fund.**  They say you can always count on 2 things in life: death and paying taxes.  I am going to add a third: emergencies.  We all have them.  Life is going to happen and we need to be prepared.  If you think you can own a car and nothing will ever go wrong, you are very mistaken.  You need an emergency fund in order to make life happening an inconvenience instead of a tragedy.  In recent years, many people have lost their jobs.  I know people who had a 3-6 month emergency fund that were able to turn that experience into a blessing and get a better job because they were not desperate.  Then there are people who had nothing and had to take any job they could and still haven't found the right job because they are too busy working the wrong one.  As fast as you can, get a 6-8 month emergency fund.  We were always taught in Girl Scouts - "Be prepared."

VII.  **Thou shalt save for retirement.**  Once you are out of debt and have your 6-8 month emergency fund, you need to begin putting 15% of your income into retirement.  You want to be able to retire before you are 80 and retire with some dignity. Social Security is not your answer and there is no government program that will help you. You need to take control of your future and save for your retirement.

VIII. **Thou shalt give.** Giving is essential for wealth. But you cannot give the way you want or should as long as you owe other people. So decide today to get out of debt, start saving for retirement, and give, give, give. Remember to change your priority order. Give first, then save and then spend. Nothing will make you happier.

IX. **Thou shalt always have integrity.** You must always be honest with yourself and your spouse about your finances. If you are deceiving yourself, or telling yourself it will be okay when you are living paycheck to paycheck, you are not being honest. And you cannot fix a problem until you are first honest about the problem. Over 50% of couples have admitted to being unfaithful to their spouses about money. You must always tell the truth and work on your finances together. The most common trait found in all millionaires is integrity. It is essential for life and for wealth.

X. **Thou shalt always have hope.** Have hope in yourself. Make sure your hope is in the right place. Don't put your hope in a government program, or the lottery. Put your hope in yourself and God. You can do this money thing. You can live on less than you make. You can get out of debt. You can have money. No matter who you are. But you must have hope in the right things. Make the choices that give you freedom not that chain you down. My money is on you.

Everything in these ten commandments we have already talked about at some point or another in this book. I believe in everything in this book and I also know that everything in it is important. However, if it is all overwhelming, just start here. When you have formed habits over the years, you will not see an instant change. And I find that most people are in so deep they don't know where to start. When we are overwhelmed, we tend to do nothing. Have you ever walked into a room in your house to clean it; you can't decide where to start so you just don't do it?  I don't want you to do that with your finances.  So if you find yourself in that position, just start here.  I hope that you will make these commandments a part of your everyday financial life the same way you make the Ten Commandments a part of your everyday life.  If you do, you can't go wrong.

# U is for Unique

*I* have always wanted to be described as unique. For someone to be unique means that they are rare, one of a kind and sought after. I don't mean sought after in a prideful way, but that they have great qualities that other people wish to emulate. To me, the opposite of unique is normal. Normal is being the way you are because everybody else is that way. Normal is following the crowd even when you don't feel right or necessarily agree.

When it comes to your personal finances, you always want to strive to be unique. In a moment, I am going to show you how a normal person handles their finances and how a unique person handles their finances. I sincerely hope after looking at both ways that you will make a decision to become more unique in your personal finance world.

I want to let you know up front that it takes a lot of effort to be a unique person. To be unique means you have to make your own decisions based on the information you have and not always go with the crowd. To be unique means you will need patience and take your time making the right decisions and not always do what is easy. To be unique means you will need to be proud of your decisions and stand behind them and not change your mind when your family and friends make fun of you. To be unique means not taking the easy way out and not doing what everyone else is doing. This is what makes you unique.

### *Normal vs. Unique*

I want you to be unique when it comes to your personal finances. But in order for you to make the move from normal to unique, you have to be convinced that unique is better. The best way I know to do that is to show you the finances of a normal person and then show you those same finances of a unique person. So here goes. Below are some facts and information on how a normal person handles their finances:

* Normal people live paycheck to paycheck.
* Normal people have very little, if anything, invested towards retirement.
* Normal people do not have any kind of savings account including an emergency fund.

- Normal people do not have a 6-8 month emergency fund to cover a job loss.
- Normal people do not give because they have nothing left at the end of the month.
- Normal people have at least one car payment and usually have two.
- Normal people use student loans to go to college and spend 30 years paying them back.
- Normal people have credit cards and use them to buy everything they want and can't wait for.
- Normal people owe every single penny they make to someone else, leaving nothing for them.
- Normal people have a mortgage more than 30% of their take home pay and many times the monthly payment does not include the insurance and the taxes.  These items bring their payments up to around 50% of their take home or more.
- Normal people are never happy and are always stressed about money.  They also are too worried about their finances to love and enjoy their spouse and kids.
- Normal people work to live.  They most likely work in jobs that they cannot stand and have no desire to do.

❖ Normal people give their kids everything they ask for and never say no to them.

❖ Normal people solve money issues with debt. When something breaks, they use debt to get another one instead of fixing it. When they are in a bind, they use debt to get out.

❖ Normal people are disorganized and do not pay attention to their money, incoming or outgoing.

Now, let's look at how a unique person handles their finances.

❖ Unique people are balanced in how they distribute their income. They distribute it between giving, saving and spending.

❖ Unique people invest around 15 – 18% of their income every month in order to support them when they retire. They do not depend on Social Security at all. If they receive Social Security at the age of 65, it will be gravy for them.

❖ Unique people have an emergency fund of at least 6-8 months of expenses and usually have some money in a money market as extra liquid savings.

❖ Unique people give and are always looking for new ways to give. Many give a percentage of their income first before they do anything else with their money.

❖ Unique people drive cars that might not always be pretty, but are paid for. Unique people also place themselves in a position to pay cash for a new car when they are ready. They never finance or lease vehicles.

❖ Unique people go to college only if they need to in order to do what they are passionate about. If they decide to go to college, they do so in a way that can be cash flowed without any loans. They also spend many hours searching and applying for every scholarship and grant they can find.

❖ Unique people do not have a credit card balance.

❖ Unique people never owe anyone. They do not have any debt and will only buy something if they can afford it and pay cash for it.

❖ Unique people rent until they can afford a mortgage that is no more than 25% of their take home pay including taxes and insurance. They also only buy once they have 20% down and of course they are already out of debt and have an emergency fund to cover anything that will go wrong.

❖ Unique people are happy and are not stressed about money. They feel very much in control of their finances and when something happens, it is an inconvenience not a tragedy. They have great marriages and a great relationship with their kids.

- ❖ Unique people love their job. They are doing what they love to do everyday. They live to work because they love what they do.
- ❖ Unique people know how to say no to their kids when necessary. They take the time to teach their kids about money, what it takes to obtain it and wise choices to make once you have it. They do not give their kids everything they want and they teach them the difference in needs and wants.
- ❖ Unique people never use debt to solve their problems. They think out the problem, look at all of their choices, and take the time to make the wisest choice possible.
- ❖ Unique people are very organized and know exactly where every dollar they make is going. They pay attention to every aspect of their personal finances.

From age 19 until about 15 years ago, when I hit bottom, I was a normal person. I did everything you could possibly do wrong with money. I made every bad choice you could make with money and those choices kept making me more and more desperate. When I was making these bad decisions, I didn't even realize how bad they were because so many other people were doing what I was doing. And even though I had unique people all around me, I couldn't see how different their life was from mine. When I hit bottom and decided to not be normal anymore, I really opened my eyes to what unique could look like and who I wanted to be. I didn't want to be normal anymore. That didn't work for me and wasn't working for other people either. I have been everything on both of the lists above. For 10 years, I lived every single item listed above for normal people. And all that did was dig me into a hole I almost couldn't get out of. But by the grace of God, I did. From that moment on, I have lived using all of the items listed above for unique people. If I can do it, you can too. Having been both normal and unique, you can trust me completely when I say, choose unique. Unique will get you ridiculed and laughed at. But unique gives you freedom, peace and choices. Remember, normal people will not be around and will not bail you out when being normal catches up with you. Choose to be unique today.

# V is for Vision

*O*ur vision is how we see things. It is the lens through which we view everything in our lives. We have a vision for our careers, for our kids, for our country, for our marriages, and for our personal finances. But our vision is not only our future. It is also our past and our present. If you only look ahead, you will miss learning from your past and living in today. Take time, before you move forward in this chapter, to be honest about the vision of your life right now. For this exercise only, since our life is a movie not a picture, take a picture of your life right now and be honest about how you view your past, your present and your future. Doing this exercise will help you see more clearly where you have been and what you can learn from that journey, where you are now and how you can best handle it and where you are going and how to make the best of it.

### *Our 20/20 World*

People are always saying "Hindsight is 20/20", which is a true statement. It is always easier to see what you should have done after the smoke has cleared. But we don't want our goal to be to only have 20/20 vision after it is too late. We want to have 20/20 vision in our present circumstances and in our future as well. But how can we do that when we have no idea of what will happen next?

First, let me start by saying you will never have perfect, 20/20 vision on your future because you don't know what will happen and you can't control other people even though you can control your actions. But we want to always do everything we can to make right decisions in our lives in order to get as close to 20/20 as we can. Let's look at what a 20/20 world looks like not only in hindsight (our past), but in our present and our future.

❖ **The Past** - The past is the past. It has happened, you can't change it, and you don't have to be defined by it. But you definitely can learn from it. You can not only learn from your past but from the past of others as well. A mistake can be a great thing if you learn from it. But too many of us keep making the same mistakes over and over. Use your 20/20 vision to identify your mistakes and the steps needed to not make them again.

❖ **The Present** – The present is here. You only get one chance in this moment. Therefore, it is imperative that you make sure that you gather all of the information you can and make the most knowledgeable, wise decisions you can. You cannot worry about tomorrow today. You need to focus on today and making the right decisions because everything you do today will affect your tomorrow. Use your 20/20 vision to make sure you are controlling what you can control and making the best decisions with the knowledge you have.

❖ **The Future** – The future will be here in a moment. You need to always have a vision of what you want your future to look like, whether you are talking about tomorrow or 5 years from tomorrow. You will get no where without vision. Use your 20/20 vision to keep dreaming and establishing future goals based on what you know today. Don't worry about tomorrow. God gives us the grace we need day by day; therefore, He won't give us tomorrow's grace today. However, you need to always have a vision of where you want to go tomorrow and be willing to change as your vision begins to focus.

We always need to have the clearest vision possible in order to make knowledgeable, wise decisions. Every decision we make has a place in our future. Hopefully your new saying will be "Today is 20/20."

### *You and Your Vision*

Your vision, again past, present and future, is your story. We will talk a lot more about your story in a couple of chapters from now. But for now, let me remind you that you are the author of your story. You get to decide your vision for your life, how you look at your life before, now and going forward. Let me ask you a question. Do you focus on the donut or the hole? Whatever your goals are, always keep your eye or your vision on the donut and not the hole. Keep your vision on what is there and can be obtained not on what is not there or missing.

With every client I work with, one of the first things we talk about is what they want for the future and why they came to me. The past is over and they can learn from it, but I want them to focus on their future first. This is the part they can change, but it won't change without a clear vision and clear goals as to what they want their story to look like.  Here is a sample of the most common visionary goals that I get.

- ❖ We want to get out of debt.
- ❖ We want to have money when we retire.
- ❖ We want to send our kids to college.
- ❖ We want to stop living paycheck to paycheck.
- ❖ We want to buy a house or get a bigger house.
- ❖ We want to have money in savings for emergencies.

These are all common goals and very basic, which is a great place to start.  But you have to have a more specific, detailed vision for your finances in order to achieve the goals.  More importantly, you have to believe in your vision or you will not be willing to do what it takes to reach these goals.  If your finances are in a mess, there will be a lot of pain in order to reach these goals.  And reaching goals takes time and a lot of hard work and dedication.  But the end result is always worth the pain.

As I am writing this, the summer Olympics are just wrapping up.  As ordinary people, we have no idea what these athletes have gone through for one chance at a medal.  Most of them have been training in their sport since they were very young.  They would get up everyday and practice before and after school and on weekends. Their families sacrificed time and finances so that they could just pursue their dream. From the time they could begin to dream, they dreamed of one day going to the Olympics. And for every one that made it, there are many who didn't. The common story among every athlete is they had a dream and they did whatever it took to reach that dream.

You must have dreams and visions. Without them, you have nothing to work for or look forward to. Without them, you will wake up in 10 years exactly where you are today. You deserve everything you want, not in an entitlement way, but in a way that God loves you and wants you to be happy. But there are many obstacles that get in the way of our dreams.

- ❖ Debt
- ❖ Self-Pity
- ❖ Jealousy (both ours and other people's)
- ❖ Doubt
- ❖ Ambition

These are just a few of the common ones. You need to remove the obstacles that are in your way and go after your dreams. "Live beyond your dreams and below your means." The biggest obstacle people have right now is debt. Most people with debt never reach their dreams. When you are in debt, you can't have the career you want. You cannot pursue your passion because you need your j-o-b to pay your bills. As long as you are giving your money away to banks and other institutions, you will never be able to use it to reach your vision for your life. Amazingly, however, many times I see people remove the debt and the rest of their obstacles just begin to fall away. It takes great courage, strength, discipline, sacrifice, and focus to get out of debt. It will also take time. But you must never give up. The athletes in this year's Olympics didn't give up and neither will the athletes who didn't make it this year. They will keep training and try again in four years.

Having vision affects your attitude. Without vision, you naturally have a pessimistic attitude toward life and your future. But with vision, your attitude is optimistic and positive. We covered in the very beginning of this book how important a positive attitude is in life and in your personal finances. Many people think they have to wait until their circumstances are perfect and they are happy in order to dream. Your circumstances will never be perfect. And there is no key to happiness. The door is always open and you can enter no matter what your circumstances. Start today to have dreams and visions and begin to remove any obstacle that prevents you from having everything you envision.

> *"For I know the plans I have for you, declares the Lord, plans to prosper you and not to harm you, plans to give you hope and a future."*
>
> *Jeremiah 29:11*

# W is for Wisdom

*W*isdom is defined as taking knowledge and making good judgments with that knowledge. I also define wisdom as thinking and using common sense. You must use some form of wisdom when it comes to your personal finances. If you make financial decisions based on what everyone else is doing or based on feelings, for example, you will most likely make a bad financial decision.

Wisdom is the area between wrong and the real world. There are financial decisions that you know are wrong, but you do them anyway. Debt is one of these decisions. Everyone knows that it is not wise to pay $21,000 for a $15,000 car. But when you finance a car, that is exactly what you are doing. Everyone knows that taking 30 years to pay for a college education is not wise, but yet everyone is doing it. As years have gone by and debt is everywhere, we have lost our wisdom and our common sense.

You do not learn about money and the wisdom of money by accident. You must learn about money on purpose. Why would you choose to learn the unwise way to handle your personal finances? You wouldn't. Yet people make money mistakes everyday and many of them over and over. Why does this happen? I believe a large part of it is lack of knowledge and lack of thinking decisions through. If you are just going through life, making big financial decisions willy nilly, you are going to make mistakes. You must take the time to think through your decisions, find the wisdom, and use common sense when it comes to personal finances or you will never obtain wealth. Wealthy people are not willy nilly people. They are on purpose people who think.

### Think This Through

You need to think about what you are thinking about. Doing this will always have you thinking and that is a good thing. You need to think in longer blocks of time. In other words, think past Friday. Author Suzy Welch wrote a book entitled "10-10-10" where she talks about how you have to look at your decisions through three eyes:

- ❖ What are the consequences of my decision in 10 minutes?
- ❖ What are the consequences of my decision in 10 months?
- ❖ What are the consequences of my decision in 10 years?

Using these three questions when making financial decisions can help you to make wiser decisions because it causes you to think beyond 10 minutes from now. Let's use this formula to have a thinking discussion about taking out student loans.

- ❖ The consequence of taking out a student loan in 10 minutes is nothing.
- ❖ The consequence of taking out a student loan in 10 months is nothing.
- ❖ The consequence of taking out a student loan in 10 years is substantial. I will be making an average payment of $250 or more for at least 10 years or more. During this time, I will have less money to save, spend and give due to this monthly obligation. And if I am unable to get a good paying job right away, this will be harder to pay back and will possibly put me behind in other things.

This is why most people go into debt. The consequences of debt are usually not immediate. When using this formula, the 10 minutes and even the 10 months are usually without consequence. But when you begin to think beyond right now and into the future, you can see what the consequences might be. You have to think beyond right now and what you can do right now. You never know what tomorrow holds. You should not make promises today that you don't know if you can keep tomorrow. Poor people ask how much down and how much per month. Wealthy people ask how much. This is because they think beyond Friday, pay cash for purchases, and live within their current means.

It is important that you not only think, but that you are a critical thinker. The definition of critical thinking is thinking that clarifies goals, examines assumptions, discerns hidden values, evaluates evidence, accomplishes actions, and assesses conclusions. To be a critical thinker means basically that you think something to death, from every side in order to make the best decision possible. Being a critical thinker also means you are an independent thinker. You do not think something just because someone else thinks it. You make up your own mind even if it is different from everyone else.

The best example I have of being a critical thinker actually isn't financial. It is political, but it will make the best point. Do you make up your mind regarding political issues based on your party or based on your true opinion? I hear so many people today simply repeating what they heard on the news as their opinion or their belief. They are mad about something, but they can't tell you why exactly. They can only repeat what someone else said. I do not care what party you belong to or who you are going to vote for. But I do care that you vote for the person that you believe is truly the best for the job. Take the time to research the facts (and there are websites that post just the facts not opinions). Actually take the time to read a bill or a law before you get mad about it. Here is a surprising fact. News programs are just scripts. Different channels are in favor of different parties; therefore, everything you hear from them is going to be one sided. I am not making a political statement. I am asking you to learn to become a critical, independent thinker. This may mean you have to go outside the box sometimes. But that is okay.

You work too hard for your money to just do what everyone else is doing. You work too hard for your money to just throw it away. Take the time to think about your money decisions and always be thinking beyond the moment. Thinking is not a guarantee for not making mistakes, but it will help you to not keep making the same mistakes over and over. "Making mistakes is good, just make new ones." Tim Sanders

### Making Common Sense Common Again

Have you ever met a person who was very book smart, but they just didn't have common sense? Common sense is what you know you should do, whether you do it or not. Common sense is just practical knowledge and judgment we have to help us to do what is best for us. Somehow, over time, we seem to have lost a lot of our common sense. We make decisions, including financial ones, based on feelings more than on what we know to be the best thing for us.

I hope that common sense will become common again, and soon. My grandparents and even my parents used practical common sense when it came to making decisions, financial and the like. They knew that spending more than you make was not good for them and they had the sense to not do that. They knew that the only way they would have money in the future was to save in the now and they had the sense to do that. They were happy with a house that they could afford and they had the sense to only buy that house. They knew that if they didn't have the cash to pay for something that meant they couldn't afford it and they had the sense to not get it and wait.

Let me ask you a question. Do you think it is better to have money for the future or to have things? When you look up in 10 years, do you want to have money in the bank or stuff in your driveway and house? I know you are not stupid and I know that you have common sense. And I know that you would rather have money in both situations, not things. Let's make decisions that are good for us and our future and not what feels good. Let's begin today to make common sense common again.

> "Common sense in an uncommon degree is what the world calls wisdom."
>
> Samuel Taylor Coleridge

# X is for X-Ray

*A* n x-ray is used to see what is going on inside. You cannot hide anything in an x-ray. It exposes everything. Sometimes in order to fix a problem, we have to start on the inside and go out. That is usually the case with our personal finances. So let's take a minute to take an x-ray of ourselves when it comes to our finances. Remember, in this exercise, like all of the others, you have to be completely honest or they won't work. Without honesty nothing will change. Now let's look inside and see what is going on.

- ❖ Why am I giving all of my hard earned money away and especially to corporations that I know are greedy in how they handle their customers?
- ❖ Until this point, what has stopped me from saving money for retirement?
- ❖ Why am I so scared to do a budget or to say no to myself and my kids? Why do I keep saying yes to things even when I know it will hurt me eventually?

- ❖ Why do I care so much what other people think? I know they aren't going to be around when I get stuck.

- ❖ Why do I overspend? What am I trying to cover up or who am I trying to please?

- ❖ What am I really angry about? Is it my spouse or my kids or is it our decisions and the way we are handling our finances?

- ❖ What is stopping me from getting out of debt? I know I want a life without debt but something is stopping me from pulling the trigger.

- ❖ Why am I so negative? I know people love me and God loves me, why can't I love myself and want the best for myself?

- ❖ What keeps me from finding the treasure in my trials? I know that everyone has stuff that doesn't go their way. There are people who have it much worse than me.

- ❖ What am I thankful for? Not just the big stuff, but even my running hot water.

- ❖ Who am I jealous of and who am I trying to emulate? Why am I doing that? Who am I and how do I let that shine?

- ❖ What are my expectations for my life? Where do I want to go and how can I get there?

❖ I want to be wealthy. What do I need to do and to change in order to get there? I know I can be just as wealthy as anyone else.

❖ Why do I choose to not pay attention when it comes to my personal finances? What am I afraid of?

❖ Why do I keep everything for myself? Am I really a generous giver or do I give out of obligation or boasting?

❖ Am I really willing to learn about the best way to handle money and make wise decisions about money? I know I won't like some of what I hear, but am I willing to learn from people who know what they are talking about because they have been there?

❖ Am I willing to listen to my spouse's opinion and let each of our votes count, even if that means I don't get my way sometimes?

❖ Do I really know the difference in my needs and my wants? Am I willing to wait for my wants and put my real needs first?

❖ I know I need to do something different but why? What am I aiming for?

❖ Why do I really want to help my kid or relative when they come to me asking me to give them money?  Am I really helping or making the problem worse?

❖ Do I like being normal?

❖ Do I really take the time to think out my decisions? Why don't I think for myself instead of saying what other people say?  Am I afraid of being rejected or wrong?

❖ Am I going to be the problem or the solution?

This is only a handful of the questions you can ask yourself about what is going on on the inside.  Remember a few chapters ago we talked about the why and that without a why you won't be motivated to change.  As you can see, many of these questions ask why.  The why works in more than one way.  It not only helps you get where you are going, but it will help you find out what is in your way.  Remember when I said that personal finance is 90% emotional and only 10% math.  Here is where the rubber hits the road.  You have to deal with the 90% or you will never get the 10% to work.

Emotions and feelings are great, but sometimes they just get in our way.  They can keep us from being all that we are supposed to be.  Many people in this country are not wealthy today because of what is on the inside, not because of their circumstances on the outside. You can grow up poor as a church mouse and become a billionaire, if you want to. It is up to you.

I had the distinct honor a couple of years ago of meeting Ms. Oprah Winfrey. Oprah was born into poverty to a single mother in Mississippi and was raised in the inter-city of Milwaukee. Oprah is the perfect example of what happens when you won't give up on yourself. She had a very rough childhood, but chose not to let that define her. She won a contest in high school that secured her a scholarship to college. She worked as a teenager in a local radio station and the rest is history.

Oprah is now a billionaire and is considered one of the top influential people of all time. I believe the two mains keys to her success are perseverance and believing in herself. She didn't let other people define who she would become. She decided who she wanted to be and didn't let anything get in her way. But if she wasn't honest with herself and know herself from the inside out, she wouldn't be where she is today.

Don't be afraid of what is on the inside. Don't be afraid to ask the tough questions and give the tough answers.

Doing this will not only change your finances, but will change you. Let the real you come out. It's time.

> "For everyone of us that succeeds, it's because there's somebody there to show you the way out."
>
> Oprah Winfrey

# Y is for You

*Y*ou are the answer. You can do anything you want to do and be anything you want to be. If you want to be wealthy, you can be wealthy. If you want to get out of debt, you can get out of debt. If you want to own your own business, you can own your own business. You are the answer.

So many great people believe that someone or something else is the answer. They think they can only be wealthy if they win the lottery. They believe they will never get out of debt. They think that they will never have any other job than the one they have right now. But I am here to tell you, you are the answer. As the end of this book is nearing, I really hope that you have learned a lot and have gained knowledge you didn't have and some courage that may have been hiding. But if you take nothing else from this book, please know this. You are the answer.

The change needed in this country is not going to come from Washington or from your state and local leaders. The change is going to come from you (and from me).

This country is angry. I see it everyday in dealing with people. I see it in the way people talk to each other and about each other. I see it in the way people drive. I see it in the way people move through a store with a shopping cart. I see older people who are so mad about everything. No one is respectful of each other any more and it is just getting worse. Can you imagine what our children are going to be like in 10 or 20 years? I don't want to imagine it. I'd rather be the change people see. If we change on a personal level, eventually others will change and so will Washington because we will vote in a way that is best for our country, not just out of anger.

You are the author of your own story. How do you want your story to read over the next couple of chapters? Do you want it to be full of stress, anger, hatred, and disrespect? Or do you want it to be full of peace, joy, happiness, love and respect? You get to decide. No one can decide for you. I know some of you aren't going to believe me and you are saying "but Debbi, you don't know my story." I do not need to know your story to know that you can be whoever you want to be. Your circumstances do not make you who you are. You do.

# You and Your Finances

If your finances were a word problem, which way would they read?

> *Tom and Pam have a take home pay of $4000 per month. The total of their monthly expenses is $4300 per month. How much more a month do they need just to make their bills?*

OR

> *Tom and Pam have a take home pay of $4000 per month. The total of their monthly expenses is $3200 per month. How much do they have left over every month to save, give and invest?*

Now, which word problem would you like your finances to read like? Again, you get to decide. You are in control of your expenses. You decide where you are going to live, what you are going to drive, how many outfits and shoes you are going to own, what you eat for dinner and so on. You can make your budget whatever you want it to be. If you choose a high lifestyle, you are going to need a high income. If you make that choice with a low income, you are going to always struggle. If you lose your job, you decide whether you will do anything to make money until the job you want comes around or if you are going to do nothing and complain. You also decide whether you are going to save money in case of a job loss or just hope nothing happens and you'll deal with it when it does.

Are you seeing my point here? I know you want to blame something or someone else for your financial position because that is easier than realizing the truth. You are in control, you make your own decisions, and you will either reap or suffer because of them. Knowing this can change your world. Knowing this can open your eyes to a whole new world where you are in control and in charge. And who doesn't want to be in charge?

### *I Don't Feel Like It*

How many times do you hear this from your kids? How many times to you say this to yourself or your spouse? You cannot run your life based on your feelings or you will never get anywhere. Think of someone famous that you admire. Do you really believe that they got to where they are today by only doing something when they felt like it? There have been many days that I haven't felt like writing. I was either tired, busy, or just having a blah day. But I knew that my dream of finishing this book and getting you this information would never come true if I didn't sit down and write anyway, even if it was just a page or two.

This is a form of discipline. You need discipline in order to make your goals and dreams come true. I will be honest here. You would be hard pressed to find someone who wants and feels like paying attention to their finances. To do so takes time, thinking, patience, and hard decision making. It is so much easier just to do what we feel like doing and hope that it works. But as many of you have seen, as I did, that way of handling money doesn't work and has very painful consequences. I hope you will make a decision, before it is too late, to fight through your feelings of not wanting to do it and do it anyway. You will feel better in the long run and end up wealthy in the process.

A woman I admire greatly and consider a friend, even though I've never had the privilege of meeting her, Joyce Meyer, wrote a new book recently entitled "Living Beyond Your Feelings: Controlling Emotions So They Don't Control You." In it she talks about just this very thing. She teaches you how to not let your feelings control your life and keep you from becoming all God wants you to be.

She teaches you to make decisions based on wisdom and balance, not feelings such as anger or rejection. If you believe that feelings are a large obstacle keeping you from writing your story, get her book to help you out.

You are always going to be fighting between what culture wants and encourages you to do and what you know you should do. Culture is a lot like a 4th of July sparkler. It is awesome for a minute and then it is gone. When you live the way other people want you to live, it might feel great in the moment, but it will quickly lose it's sparkle as you have to deal with the consequences. Doing the right thing and being all that you want to be is an every day, every minute process. It is easy to begin a diet on Sunday night. Monday morning is when the true test comes. And then Tuesday and Wednesday, and so on. We all want to get out of debt and be financially secure, but the only way you can be is to make a lifestyle change, a daily decision to do what is right, not what culture or your feelings want.

It is easy to commit when we are in trouble, but it is hard to stay committed and to change our lifestyle. But I know you can do it. I know this because I did it and if I can, you can too. You have to take charge, today, of your life and your story. You have to decide what you want in life and go about doing what you need to get it. You need to stop listening to everyone around you and make the decisions that you know are right. You are the answer. You are the solution. You can be anybody that you want to be.

> "You can suffer the pain of change or suffer remaining the way you are."
>
> *Joyce Meyer*

# Z is for Zoie Lovell King

*I* thought that Z would be the hardest letter of all, but it turns out it was the easiest. Zoie Lovell King was my paternal grandmother and the best example of how to live your life in every way, not just financial. But she was a great example there as well. She passed away in 2000 at the age of 102. I truly believe that the reason she lived to this awesome age was her attitude about life. I would like to share just some of her thoughts and attitudes with you so that you can get to know her and love her, like so many others did.

❖ Zoie always put everyone else before herself. Not just her husband, kids and grandkids, but friends and strangers alike. I cannot remember one time hearing a selfish word come out of her mouth.

❖ Zoie was happy no matter what the circumstances were in her life. Her and my grandfather lived through the depression, lived through my grandfather being overseas during WWI, lived through having 10 kids, losing 3 and raising 7.

They lived through leaving family to move to Florida so my grandfather could work for the railroad. My grandmother lived through burying her husband and 2 adult children. My grandparents lived through selling their home so that their daughter could have an operation, renting for a short while and then buying again. And these are just a few of the circumstances they went through. During this time, my grandmother never gave up, never lost her faith, and never complained.

❖ Zoie never wanted for anything. She was always happy with what she had and was very happy to have it. Ever since I can remember, she was always embarrassed to receive any gift she received. She was always grateful, but she always thought the money should have been spent on someone else.

❖ Zoie was a simple lady and truly enjoyed her simple life. My grandmother, from when I can remember, hardly went anywhere except to church. But nothing made her happier than to spend time with her grandchildren and to crochet. I would usually spend a week or two with her in the summer when I was younger and she would crochet and watch me play and she did this with a smile on her face the whole time. She loved to spoil her grandchildren, but it was with simple things like watching television or making cookies, not with expensive things.

These are just a few of the things that I loved and admired about my grandmother. She is who I try to emulate each and every day. She is an example for everyone to follow and that is why I have dedicated this last chapter to her.

### *Back to the Future*

I want to take a few minutes to go back in time, starting with my grandmother's time, to remind everyone of where we came from and I hope it will help us have a different vision of where we want to go. A lot of things, both good and bad, have happened in the past and many of the good things that we should have kept and should live by went away. We are going to make 4 stops on our journey and I hope that we can take away some new lessons from each stop.

# First Stop – 1920-1930

❖ My maternal grandparents were an example of how many people earned a living and saved during this time. They were farmers whose crops came in from May to September. Therefore, they had to spread out their income from October to April and save in case they had a bad crop year. If they didn't budget and manage their money correctly, they would be in great trouble since there weren't credit cards and loans to get them through.

❖ They only had one car per family and that was all they needed.

❖ They had radios and the family would gather around and listen.

❖ They ate simply, mostly what they grew or baked. They would trade if they needed something they didn't have.

❖ Christmas was usually one present and usually something that they made.

❖ There was no credit available except maybe at the local store and this was simply a charge until you got paid. They had to save for everything.

### Second Stop – 1950-1960

❖ My parents, aunts, and uncles are an example of living in this time. People began to leave the farms and go get jobs once they finished high school. There was a lot of industry around as more and more things became available.

❖ This generation took their money education from their parents, but they made more money. Therefore, they were able to save a lot more. They were still content with what they had. For example, most homes only had one television even though they may have had the money for more.

❖ This is the time when the universal credit card became available, starting with the Diners Club designed for salesman and it expanded from there. It started with charge cards, with no interest, being paid off every month. And then in the 1960's, credit cards, with interest for balances carried from month to month, became available

❖ Lots of things were becoming more affordable and available.

### Third Stop – 1980-1990

❖ Credit is everywhere. Enough said.

❖ People wanted everything immediately and could get it because of credit. This is how my nightmare began in 1990. As I have told you before I wanted everything my parents had the day I graduated from college. I didn't want to wait to save for it like they did.

❖ This generation, my generation, learned discipline from our parents and grandparents, but many of us decided we knew better. And thus the journey of losing control of our personal finances began.

❖ College was a privilege that not everyone had. College was valued by the student and was paid for mostly in cash by the money that their parents had worked hard to save.

❖ This is when I believe the age of discontentment began because people started to become more aware that there was better out there.

### Final Stop – Today

❖ We must have everything now. We only want the biggest and the best because that is what we "deserve".

❖ We do not care about the future. We believe that there is always time to save and invest and the future will take care of itself.

❖ We have a huge entitlement attitude, meaning we are to be given everything just because. Everything is ours to have or take without thought of others or our future.

❖ Debt is not a problem (in our minds). As long as we can make the monthly payment, we can "afford" it. Today is all that matters. It doesn't matter whether I can afford the payment in 2 years or in 2 months. It is about right now.

❖ We look at college as a right whether you can afford it or not. Again, we are entitled and deserve a college education and we will worry about paying for it later because, of course, we will get the perfect job the day we graduate from college.

## Solutions for the Future

❖ Take savings and money education from our grandparents and parents and use it today. Their way of handling money never goes out of style.

❖ You can still have what you want and have more than our grandparents and parents ever dreamed of. You just need to wait until you can afford it.

❖ You have to save for your own future. Government programs will eventually cease to exist and then what will you do? Take care of yourself.

❖ Be the author of your own story and stop keeping up with the Jones's. Stop being someone you are not.

❖ Dream your passion and live it. Be everything that you want to be and more.

This chapter has been my favorite to write because it allowed me to talk about my favorite person in the whole world, my grandmother. When I filed for bankruptcy many years ago and had to start over, I went to three places to learn how to handle money: the Bible, my parents, and my grandmother. I didn't know a lot of details about her and my grandfather's finances, but I knew they weren't great. But her attitude was. She found joy and happiness in everything but money. Stuff meant nothing to her, people did. I hope that when I am 102, people will be able to say the same about me. I hope you all have grandparents and parents that you can look to to help you through your financial journey, but if you don't, please feel free to use my grandmother. It would put a smile on her face to see one on yours.

> "A good name is more desirable than great riches; to be esteemed is better than silver or gold."
>
> *Proverbs 22:1*

***Please visit Debbi anytime at***
***www.abcsofpersonalfinance.com.***

*She is always available to anyone, no matter where you live, to answer your questions, to coach you and to personalize a plan for you to get on the right road for your journey.*

*Doing nothing will never move your forward.*

41586140R00175

Made in the USA
Lexington, KY
08 June 2019